1962

This book may be kept

AMERICAN CATHOLIC DILEMMA

An Inquiry into the Intellectual Life

AMERICAN CATHOLIC DILEMMA: *An Inquiry into the Intellectual Life*

by THOMAS F. O'DEA

Introduction by
GUSTAVE WEIGEL, S.J.

SHEED AND WARD · NEW YORK

© Sheed & Ward, Inc., 1958

Library of Congress Card Number 58-5887

O'Dea, Thomas F
    American Catholic dilemma: an inquiry into the intel-
lectual life. Introd. by Gustave Weigel. New York,
Sheed and Ward [1958]
    173 p.   22 cm.
    Includes bibliography.

1. Catholics in the U. S.   2. U. S.—Intellectual life.   i. Title.

BX1407.I 5O3   282.73   58–5887 ‡

Library of Congress

Manufactured in the United States of America

To my Mother

Acknowledgements

The analytical framework upon which this book is based owes much to the work of two important sociologists, Talcott Parsons of Harvard University, who was my teacher, and the late Karl Mannheim.

I also want to thank all those who encouraged my efforts: the Very Reverend Laurence J. McGinley, S.J., President of Fordham University, who upon seeing a preliminary draft was the first to suggest publication; Rev. Gustave A. Weigel, S.J.; Rev. Vincent Martin, O.S.B.; my colleagues at Fordham, Professors Charles Donahue and Frank A. Santopolo, and many others both at Fordham and elsewhere. Responsibility for final interpretations in this work rests, of course, entirely with me.

Special thanks are owed to Philip Scharper, a patient and helpful editor, and to my wife who both aided and encouraged me.

Thomas F. O'Dea

Fordham University
June 1958

"And the Lord appeared to Solomon in a dream by night, saying: Ask what thou wilt that I should give thee. And Solomon said . . . Give . . . to thy servant an understanding heart. . . . And the Lord said to Solomon: Because thou hast asked this thing, and hast not asked for thyself long life or riches, nor the lives of thy enemies, but hast asked for thyself wisdom to discern judgment, behold I have done for thee according to thy words . . . and the things also which thou didst not ask, I have given thee."

3 Kings, 3:3, 6, 9, 11-13

Contents

ix

Introduction

By this time everyone knows that there is a warm discussion going on in American Catholic circles concerning the state of intellectual endeavor among American Catholics. Fortunately, non-Catholics have politely and wisely kept out of the debate. In consequence, the dialogue has remained purely domestic, as it should be.

It all began simply enough. In 1946 there was formed The Catholic Commission on Intellectual and Cultural Affairs. The motive for this action was a certain amount of social pressure brought to bear on American Catholics by the work of the Pax Romana association of Europe, which was a Catholic organization for all Catholics engaged in intellectual work. The association had no intention of being merely European and wanted American cooperation. In the European cadres of Pax Romana, university students were most conspicuous. In America it was felt that the many Catholic colleges and universities, along with the national federation of Newman Clubs, took care of this phase of Catholic action. However, a professors' union was considered to be feasible and helpful. Hence it was given form and being.

The group, which as late as 1958 does not count 300 members, was ever gentle and harmless enough. They certainly felt no vocation toward revolt or intrigue. Actually they are not very active. They hold regional meetings and one annual national convention. So far not much more has been done than to hold meetings for discussions. There is no organ of publication. The Group has no subsidy. The first Executive Director chosen was the Rev. Edward Stanford, O.S.A., who kept his post until 1953, when his obligations to his own Order made it impossible for him to carry on the work of the Commission. At his suggestion, the Commission then chose the Rev. William Rooney, Ph.D., professor at the Catholic University of America, as the Executive Director. He has spearheaded the work since 1954. In spite of the fact that the Directors have always been clerics, the Commission is conceived as a layman's organization. Every Chairman (elected for one year) so far has been a layman.

In early 1955, as preparation for the national convention, there was a regional meeting scheduled for the Washington-Baltimore area. The meeting was held at Georgetown University and was chaired by Msgr. John Tracy Ellis, professor of American Church History at Catholic University. He was to give an address at the annual convention of 1955 on the state of American Catholic Intellectualism. The group discussed the theme and later Msgr. Ellis wrote his paper, which he delivered at St. Louis.

This discourse caused an immediate stir. Under the title "The American Catholic and the Intellectual Life" it was published in the quarterly *Thought* [30 (1955), 351-388] and reprinted extensively. Since the topic evoked vital response, the Commission decided to stay with the theme. Hence the 1956 meeting at New York devoted its session to further meditation on the problem.

For the 1957 meeting Dr. Thomas O'Dea, Associate Professor of Sociology at Fordham University, was asked to give a sociologist's report on the issue. Dr. O'Dea did prepare a study, but its form did not lend itself to group discussion, and so the present writer was drafted to treat the question from a theologian's point of view. This work, "American Catholic Intellectualism—A Theologian's Reflections," was published in Notre Dame's *The Review of Politics* [19 (1957), 275-307]. From that point on, the discussion became general. Men like Monsignor Ellis and Father Weigel were joined by Martin Svaglic of Loyola University, Chicago, Rev. John Cavanaugh, C.S.C., and others. They were critical but in no way subversive. On the other hand, Msgr. Joseph Fenton of Catholic University and Rev. Robert I. Gannon, S.J., along with others, found themselves in disagreement with the critics.

This is where the discussion stands in the spring of 1958. In the beginning, conversations were calm and leisurely, but by this time the discussion has assumed the keen edge of debate. This is perhaps inevitable, and it is not necessarily a bad thing. It is to be hoped that the issue will be a clarification of both positions.

Professor O'Dea has revised the study he prepared for the Catholic Commission on Intellectual and Cultural Affairs. The present book is the fruit of his reflections. In the whole discussion up to this point, no study has been made with the profundity and capacity manifested in the present work. Hence this dissertation is important. That does not mean that we have now heard the last word. As Professor O'Dea points out, much of his thinking is tentative and he wishes to open up areas for research rather than offer the fruits of such investigation.

Professor O'Dea is peculiarly equipped for the task he was invited to undertake. Concerning the sincerity and depth of his Catholic allegiance there can be no doubt. His training, sharpening a keen mind, was achieved in the best intellectual centers. He was a student at Harvard, where he received his doctorate. He taught at the Massachusetts Institute of Technology. He was a fellow at the Center for Advanced Study in the Behavioral Sciences at Stanford. His recent book, *The Mormons* (Chicago: University of Chicago Press, 1957), proves him to be a sympathetic and sure analyst of sociological phenomena.

There will be controversy as a result of this book. That is not an evil; nevertheless there will always be those to whom controversy, and especially heated debate, is distressing. Let us therefore try to keep in mind certain things. The very fact of the present discussion is an encouraging sign of an intellectual awakening in the Catholic body. A question is being explored honestly, courageously and in good faith. It is to be hoped that no effort, however well-intentioned, will be made to suppress the debate; for suppression will not remove the problem.

Professor O'Dea makes some suggestions; refers to situations as he sees them. There will be some who will think his hypotheses untenable, the situations he describes exaggerated. They have the satisfaction of knowing that Professor O'Dea is fallible, and no one will stress this truth more than Professor O'Dea.

On another occasion I felt the need of quoting something from the writings of St. Ignatius Loyola. I would like to repeat that quotation as an *envoi* to this introduction to Professor O'Dea's sociological consideration of American Catholic intellectualism.

The presumption is that a good Christian should be more prone to save the proposition of his neighbor than to condemn it. If, indeed, he cannot save it, let him then inquire how the neighbor understands it. If this understanding of it be bad, let the Christian correct the neighbor with love. Should this be insufficient, let him take all suitable measures to make the proposition acceptable by giving it a good meaning. (*Exercitia Spiritualia, sancti patris Ignatii de Loyola. Textus hispanus et versio litteralis . . . ex editione quarta romana anni* 1852. Turin & Rome: Marietti, 1928, pp. 32,33, n. 22.)

Gustave Weigel, S.J.
Woodstock College

CHAPTER I

State of the Question

CHAPTER I

State of the Question

Recent international developments in science have focussed the attention of the American people upon the problems which are involved in education, and the place of intellectual activities in general in our national life. Yet this discussion, now so to speak in the public domain, is but an extension of an inquiry which has long been of deep concern to that portion of the public which is engaged in intellectual activities. For the processes involved in the creation, transmission and conservation of culture must constantly be the object of study, are always in need of reconsideration, critical appraisal, and reform. That this is the case may come as a surprise to the general public, looking with admiration or with suspicious bewilderment at our educational system at work; but among educators themselves it has long been a matter of common knowledge, accepted as a basis of educational theory and practice. Creative intellectuals outside the educational system as well have long been concerned with these problems. Hence the present "crisis" is but the coming into the public awareness of what has been a continuing process for those whose special concern those problems are.

In a democracy we assume, and quite rightly, that when the public becomes aware of a problem an advance has been made towards its solution. Thus, although in the present circumstances the public may at times fail to grasp the deeper aspects of the issues involved or propose well-intentioned but shortsighted solutions (such as a "crash" program to train scientific technicians), the remote consequence cannot but be a more intelligent general understanding of the special problems in this field.

Since American Catholics are an integral part of American life and of the American commonwealth, it is not surprising that they too have been engaged in this general reconsideration of the problems of the intellectual life. Yet since they also have in certain respects a separate intellectual tradition, and in fact a separate institutional context in the Catholic schools, colleges and universities of the land—a wholly unique development in Catholic history—their reconsideration has special characteristics and involves the appraisal of special problems, or at least of special aspects of the general problems which are peculiar to the Catholic community with its distinct institutions and historical experience.

As a matter of fact, Catholics had been engaged in public discussion and criticism of their part in this important area of the national life before the launching of the Russian satellite precipitated the present national controversy. Several years ago a shrewd English observer of America noted that "the Catholic Church in America has counted for astonishingly little in the formation of the American intellectual climate."[1] Calling attention to the problems of immigration and assimilation which the Church faced in the nineteenth and in the early twentieth century, he added, "Not until this generation has the Church been given time to take breath and take stock."

There were, of course, spokesmen among earlier Catholic generations. Some sixty years ago Bishop John Lancaster Spalding, speaking before the Third Plenary Council of Baltimore, called upon his fellow Catholics to raise up men "who will take their place among the first writers and thinkers of their day."[2] But other problems pressed too hard for the challenge to be met in that generation. In the 1920's George N. Shuster, who for over a generation has been an outstanding Catholic figure in American secular education—an almost lone figure, as a matter of fact—looked in vain for genuine intellectual and artistic accomplishment among American Catholics and concluded that "Catholics have not even done what might reasonably have been expected of them to foster letters, speculation and the arts."[3]

Other voices were raised, but only after the Second World War did the inquiry of isolated individuals take the form of a genuine discussion; and not until the last years of the first post-war decade did it assume broad proportions and a sense of urgency. It was dramatized in 1955 by the publication of Monsignor John Tracy Ellis' *The American Catholic and the Intellectual Life*, which intensified both public discussion and private concern. The basic problem treated by Msgr. Ellis' book was what he referred to as "the impoverishment of Catholic scholarship in this country, as well as the low state of Catholic leadership in most walks of national life."[4] His observations have been supported by others both before and since the publication of his study. A priest in New England, writing of conditions in his own section, stated that there, "perhaps more than in many other sections" of the country, "the lack of a Catholic intellectual elite is strongly felt."[5] Another Catholic priest, in referring to the strategic Middle Atlantic states, commented that despite "heavy Catholic concentration" in that region, Catholics "are still poorly represented in school administration, boards of foundations, leadership in civic organizations, literature and science."[6]

A recent sociological analysis of the occupational and class structure of American Catholics has made the point that Catholics, while rising in the world, have not shared in the general upward social mobility in proportion to their numbers.[7] Another study of *Who goes to college, and what becomes of those who do?* indicated that Catholics go to college less frequently than do Jews and Protestants and upon graduation tend to earn lower salaries and to occupy more humble positions.[8] More recently, Rev. John J. Cavanaugh, former president of Notre Dame University, stated that "The 35,000,000 Catholics in this country and our Catholic educational system are not producing anywhere near their proportion of leaders."[9] It has been possible for a Catholic sociologist to speak of "the almost complete failure of American lay Catholics to distinguish themselves in terms of scholarship."[10] The *Catholic World* for January, 1958, declared that, "The limitations of Catholic schools are revealed each time the National Science Foundation Fellowship Awards are distributed. In 1956 the Foundation gave out 775 fellowships; only seventeen went to students in Catholic colleges. In 1957 the Foundation gave out 845 fellowships; only nineteen went to students in Catholic colleges."[11]

Since Monsignor Ellis' publication served to focus the discussion, it is interesting to see what sort of response his efforts evoked. In April of 1956, he told the National Catholic Educational Association that on the whole the reactions had revealed "a substantial agreement" with his position. Of the ten editorials in the Catholic press which he himself had seen, "nine were friendly in tone and for the most part were in agreement."[12] The Boston *Pilot* "maintained that those who might wish to dispute the article's thesis could win a hearing for their case only 'when they give us names and numbers.' "[13]

The real situation is not difficult to see. The briefest survey of the various fields of intellectual endeavor confirms what the critics have been saying. How many important Catholic novelists are to be found today upon the American scene? Even if we include converts in their number, how many American Catholic poets of real quality do we have? Although our answer to the second question is more encouraging than is the answer to the first, the situation revealed speaks for itself. What of the drama? And again, with a couple of exceptions, what of drama criticism? What of music? Where are the prominent American Catholic composers, performers or critics? How many full-time departments of music do we have among our Catholic colleges and universities?*

---

* The point here, of course, is not how many creative artists we can number who are Catholics, but the number of those who are both authentically Catholic in inspiration and authentically artistic in their work.

Spain is an old Catholic country and Spanish culture is at the foundation of most of the Latin American countries, but where are the eminent Catholics in Hispanic Studies and where are our experts on Latin America? Does one go to a Catholic university to find a first-grade regional program in those areas? The Catholic tradition has been intimately connected with the development of the graphic arts, but where are the American Catholic Rouaults? Furthermore, where are the Catholic art historians? How much better have we done—or do we do—in classics, where our long tradition of humanism might have been expected to stand us in good stead? Today Western civilization is experiencing what has been called the meeting of East and West. Our contemporaries of the West are discovering Asia. The Catholic missionary in fact discovered that continent in the sixteenth century, but where are the American Catholic Orientalists? Africa is emerging into modern civilization, a development pregnant with meaning for the Church and the world, but where do we stand in African Studies? How many names come to the minds of even the best informed in connection with these areas of intellectual life? In some, one or two, or perhaps three; in others none at all.

But, it may be suggested, in view of the special religious emphasis of our educational efforts, do we not give a better account of ourselves in fields more closely allied with religious concerns? Actually there are three or four Catholic theologians who are important intellectual figures in America. The same may be said of the field of philosophy by merely changing the number to four or five. An American scripture scholar, speaking of a field where real contributions have been made, could talk of a "remarkable advance" in biblical scholarship among American Catholics, but he had to add that there was "good reason for modesty," since "there are few among us whose productions, in quantity or quality, rate with what has been done and is being done by fellow countrymen not of the Faith or by fellow Catholics in Europe."[14] One might ask what effect such scholarly advances have had upon the biblical culture of the Catholic population generally, and upon the religious education of Catholics in America. Here we would find further "reason for modesty."

In recent times the social sciences have become of tremendous importance on the intellectual scene, both within and outside the colleges and universities. How many nationally important economists and sociologists have we?

There is really nothing mysterious about the basic facts of our situation. There is a simple test that every reader may make for himself. Let him simply examine the shelves of any Catholic bookshop in this country, or let him look over the lists of Catholic books issued by American publishers. A simple count will reveal that an overwhelming proportion of the serious books on every subject are of European origin. The fact is that although American Catholics have the largest and most expensive educational system of any national Catholic group in the world, a genuine Catholic intellectual life is still dependent upon translations of European works and books of British origin. When the American Catholic reaches the point in his intellectual development at which it is necessary to change his intellectual diet from milk to meat, he by necessity becomes an importer. Those among this generation of educated American Catholics who understand either Catholic problems or general problems in Catholic terms have been nurtured largely by their own study of a handful of European authors, outstanding among whom are Maritain, Gilson, de Lubac, Marcel and Guardini. It is hardly necessary to stress these facts, because they are generally recognized by large numbers concerned with the improvement of Catholic intellectual life.

That the present situation is clearly recognized by those closely and seriously concerned with the solution of the problems it presents is to be seen in any number of readily available examples. In the Proceedings of the Fifty-third Annual meeting of the National Catholic Educational Association, held at St. Louis, Missouri, on April 3-6, 1956, a nun speaking to the meeting of the Committee on Graduate Study raised the question, "Why is the American Catholic College Failing to Develop Catholic Intellectualism?" while the dean of a leading Catholic university raised the same question with respect to the American Catholic Graduate School.[15] The nun said, among other things, that "The chief obstacle to the development of Catholic intellectualism in our colleges is, I believe, the absence of an intellectual tradition in our American Catholic population. This is true not only for the rank and file of Catholics; it is also true of our bishops and religious superiors, both men and women, who are responsible for the education and training of religious teachers and for the selection of lay teachers for all levels of our Catholic educational system."[16] Another speaker at the same general meetings declared that "American Catholic scholars have as yet created no intellectual tradition to be 'carried on.' "[17]

Yet despite the reality of the problem and the serious and honest recognition of it by those engaged in meeting it, a regrettable attitude is far too general among those who see the situation as one calling for defense of the Catholic body in its public relations. It is suggested, for example, that scholarship is a technical consideration only, and that the criticism of our lack of it is not a matter of first importance. Such criticism is indeed described as an "unfortunate" phenomenon which can profitably be ignored. Moreover, the obviously irrelevant observation is made that American Catholic life and Catholic colleges and universities need others besides intellectuals. It is charged that a bad impression is created when Catholics engage in blunt self-criticism, at least when it is done out loud. The impression is even conveyed by some commentators that "science" is irretrievably allied with "atheism," and that to ask why we have so few Catholic scientists of note is equivalent to asking why we have so few Catholic atheists. All these attempts at defense, however well-intentioned they may be, have the effect of distracting the attention of the Catholic public from the real issues and of making loyalty appear to be identified with the silencing of criticism.

One Catholic paper—the only one of ten that Monsignor Ellis found offering an unfriendly editorial response to his review of our situation—took refuge in semantics. "It is also our conviction," said this paper, "that many of those termed 'intellectuals' both here and abroad never really deserved the hero worship accorded them. After all,

what are the standards of judgment? . . . What is meant
by an intellectual anyway? Is he one who uses sesquipedal-
ian words? Is he the individual who is considered profound
because no one can understand what he's saying? Are we
to sing the praises of the individual who isolates himself
from the rest of the world, buries himself in his books, and
becomes fogbound to everything about him, while we look
down our noses at the individual who uses his God-given
talents, is highly successful in his profession, but still re-
tains the common touch? Are we to belittle the tremendous contribution of the great body of good, sound citizens
as we go about searching for a poet laureate?"[18]

Let us admit that it is easy to understand why American
Catholics, with their long history of minority status, may
react defensively to criticism which points up their shortcomings. It is even easy to sympathize with such a reaction. But when that reaction descends to anti-intellectualism—and the editorial quoted is precisely that—then
one must ask not for intellectual standards but merely for
the simple, common, sound standards of honest discussion. As the Boston *Pilot* said of those who try to evade
Monsignor Ellis' criticism by hedging on the semantic
definition of the term intellectual, "This is a ruse which
we must not allow ourselves."[19] The present healthy Catholic concern with intellectual problems presents a challenge far too serious to be evaded by ruses.

An obvious cause for such defensive reactions is the fear
of "washing dirty linen in public." Such a reaction, however, reveals a failure to grasp the realities involved. The
shortcomings which have been aired in this public discussion are already well known in circles informed about con-

ditions in intellectual life generally. A recent study of the origins of American scientists declared of Catholic educational institutions that "without exception, they lie among the least productive 10 percent of all institutions and constitute a singularly unproductive sample."[20] Another investigation stated that "we had expected that Catholic institutions would be marked by relatively large contributions to the field of humanities. In this speculation, however, we were again mistaken. Catholic institutions, though exceptionally unproductive in all areas of scholarship, achieve their best record in the sciences."[21]

The present book is not concerned with establishing the existence of the problem—it is almost too self-evident to need further documentation—but rather with the attempt to find some of its causes. It represents an effort to consider from a sociological perspective the factors which inhibit the development of an intellectual life among American Catholics. Since our main concern will be with the diagnosis of the sources of difficulty, our approach should serve to direct attention from the mere fact of the problem to the factors which must be understood if the situation is to be changed. But as a diagnosis of the sources of difficulty, we fear that it may not make pleasant reading.

Perhaps one reason why this book may disappoint some of its readers is that it will fail to meet certain unvoiced and indeed unconscious expectations which so many of us harbor. Many Catholics tend to identify critical analysis of Catholic affairs with disloyalty. This is, of course, an unthinking reaction with roots in a persecuted Catholic past; it is to be hoped that readers in this category will recognize it for what it is. Others, while they recognize the need for the rational reconsideration of social developments, have come to expect that any commentary by Catholics upon the phenomena of Catholic life will be expressed in what has become a stereotyped form. This form can be found explicitly prescribed or recommended by no authority; nevertheless it has become the standard pattern expected of the Catholic critic of Catholic affairs.

It is generally anticipated that any critical statement will devote approximately three-quarters of its space to recalling our Catholic virtues and describing our achievements in some detail; it is only in such a self-congratulatory context that a few self-critical comments, suggesting that we have our shortcomings, may be modestly inserted. Thus is the medicine diluted, the unpleasant fact made palatable. The effect is, above all, that the sense of urgency which should be conveyed is lost, and the issue is complacency.

Since it attempts to diagnose the causes of trouble, the present work must reverse such expectations. It will concentrate upon negative phenomena, upon things which inhibit our development, not upon things which inspire, elicit, direct and encourage it. It will therefore leave much unsaid. That the contributions and achievements of Catholics in American life are real is not to be denied. That the situation with respect to the very problems we are considering has recently improved seems also to be true. The positive aspects of American Catholic life are not in question: they are not extolled in these pages because they are not the issue. It is not necessary to praise health.

In view of this concentration on the sources of difficulties, some may find the approach "unfortunate." But what is really unfortunate is the situation which exists in reality and which this book is an attempt to analyze. To dress up the real situation—especially after others have so effectively laid it bare before us—would serve no great purpose. It would in fact defeat the very end of diagnosis, which is to probe to the causes of a disorder, so that it may be rectified by intelligent action.

In order to give a full account of the problems involved, the writer has had to make use of the observations of many others and to draw upon the experience of associates and colleagues. As a result this study is interpretative rather than original in terms of its sources. It is also, to a great extent, concerned with hypotheses. The analysis of many situations and problems could not be carried through to a reliable conclusion without the consideration of much more empirical data than is available at the present time. What actually has been done is to examine the general situation, as the studies and observations of others have revealed it, in terms of the conceptual instruments of sociological analysis.

On this basis hypotheses have been proposed with respect to what appear to be important factors maintaining the present conditions. The validity of such hypotheses can, of course, only be determined by further empirical research. In fact it is one of the explicit aims of this work to provide for sociologists a frame of reference not only with regard to the larger factual dimensions of the situation itself but also with regard to a sociological theory which may guide further empirical investigation. Empirical research demands some theoretical orientation if it is to be anything more than random observation. The present book attempts to offer the main outlines of such an orientation.

Yet it it to be hoped that a work of this kind will prove useful to a more general body of readers. An interpretative analysis from the perspective of sociology can throw real light upon our present problems. By doing so it can show the general reader some of the elements worthy of his consideration. Moreover, by suggesting hypotheses, it can offer him the kind of questions that sociological theory indicates as important in the assessment of the problems. And in that way some contribution can be made towards moving the general discussion to a consideration of practical solutions.

If this work can exercise even a slight influence towards that end, it will have served its purpose. For apart from the danger that the general discussion may be diverted from its purpose by defensive reactions, there is the further danger that it may degenerate into a general lament devoid of constructive, policy-making effort. Social-science analysis cannot issue in policy, for the process of policy-making involves decisions with regard to values which are beyond its scope as a science. But it can reveal the factors that must be evaluated. It is hoped that the present work, despite its tentative and hypothetical aspects—and they should be noted by the reader for what they are—will accomplish this purpose.

Its first postulate is the problematical character of the creation, transmission and conservation of culture which we have already discussed. Thus it will begin with a consideration of the problems which beset intellectual life in any society and proceed to an examination of peculiarly

Catholic problems. Finally it will narrow its focus to the problems of Catholics in the United States. It represents the perspective of one intellectual discipline, and thus, whatever its merits, it remains a partial treatment of its subject. But it is hoped that it may be a relevant contribution to the present Catholic appraisal and may make itself heard in the continuing discussion of which it is a part.

CHAPTER II

The General Problem of the Intellectual

Part 1: Status and Role of the Intellectual:
An Analysis of Ambiguities

Part 2: The Role of the Specialist: The
Structure of Suspicion

Part 3: Activism. The Disvaluation of Pure
Knowledge

Part 4: The Role of the Intellectual and the
Manifest Content of Catholic Culture
Patterns

Book Legislation: An Important
Example

CHAPTER II

The General Problem of
the Intellectual

The problem of developing an intellectual life among American Catholics should be seen as in part unique, since it is concerned with the American Catholic experience, and in part as a variant of the general problem of the intellectual life among the societies of which history and contemporary studies make us aware. In the first chapter we noted that those involved in intellectual activities are, and have long been, aware that the creation, conservation and transmission of culture are processes which require constant observation and study. Of their very nature they are characterized by certain instabilities. It will be the purpose of this chapter to examine those instabilities in their most general aspects, while in Chapter III we shall look at the special form which they assume in Catholic history.

Part 1: The Status and Role of the Intellectual: An Analysis of Ambiguities

Our first task is to decide upon a definition of the term intellectual which will serve our present needs. What is an intellectual? Obviously he is not simply one who thinks, for everybody must do some thinking. Nor is he necessarily one who thinks clearly, for the intellectual—as we have been repeatedly reminded—can be confused and bewildered. Here we shall regard as intellectuals "those men and women whose main interest is the advancement of knowledge, or the clarification of cultural issues and public problems."[1] Intellectuals, then, are those committed to the intellectual solution of human problems, and it will be noted that the term can include creative artists and critics as well. That is to say, when any institution of society—custom, tradition, loyalties, even the meaning of life itself as defined and accepted by society—is called into question by events, experience or an advance in knowledge, the intellectual insists that the issue must prove itself able to meet the test of the intellect. Thus to the intellectual belongs the role of evaluation and criticism to a much higher degree than to other members of society. It is this function of evaluation and criticism which introduces a certain ambiguity into the relations between the intellectual and his fellow men.

The intellectual, then, represents the razor's edge of creativity for his society in terms of meeting the challenge of the unknown and unstructured future. Moreover, the intellectual performs a conserving function by transmitting the accumulation of past learning to coming generations. As the agent of these functions, he is honored.

But he is also a critic of much—and potentially of all— that is accepted, since he exalts the intellect to the position of supreme arbiter and makes of the judgment the highest human function. To some degree the intellectual always embodies the dictum of Socrates that the unexamined life is not worth living. Like Socrates, who is his great prototype, he thereby exposes himself to the charge of subversion or, as it was called in Athens, impiety. Even in his conservative function as the transmitter of tradition, the intellectual often is more than a passive or neutral channel of transmission. Most frequently transmission by intellectuals is a matter that involves passing critical judgment upon the content of what is transmitted, or of estimating the genuine contributions of the past. In thereby purifying tradition he may often come into conflict with currently accepted versions, and with those who have a vested interest in preserving these versions.

When, in a society, there are individuals or groups whose status is the object of the public honor due to distinguished service, the honor accorded them is never free of suspicion; the reaction which they evoke from the society at large is ambivalent. This situation involves a psychological dimension peculiar to the intellectual's status and role. It has two aspects which are of interest. One concerns the intellectual himself; the other concerns the non-intellectual member of the same society.

So far as the intellectual himself is concerned, his commitment to the advancement of knowledge exposes him as a person to the challenge of the new and different elements which have entered into the definition of values and of the meaning of life. It exposes his beliefs to the acid test of critical reason as he confronts views which are different from, and perhaps antagonistic to, his own. He runs the risk of dissolving, by critical activity, the meaningful basis of his own life. The anxiety which results is an occupational hazard for him, and he usually has a number of partial psychological defenses against it.

Yet the intellectual most often stands in the front line of defense against the challenges which divergent or antagonistic values offer to the basic affirmations of his society. If some intellectuals are on occasion deceived by what prove to be frauds or lunatic schemes, these are the casualties to be expected from the nature of intellectual work. Those who take particular pleasure in upbraiding or ridiculing the intellectuals are often expressing more than disapproval of their specific blunders. Frequently they are displaying "over-determined" behavior; that is, while openly expressing disapproval of the concrete activities of a certain intellectual group, they are at the same time less candidly, and to some extent unconsciously, showing their hostility toward the critical side of the intellectual's function in general. Here is one important root of what is called "anti-intellectualism."

In America today some Catholics fall prey to anti-intellectualism and excoriate the intellectuals as "egg-heads." Most often, of course, they take pains to point out that they are in favor of "real" intellectuals, but in view of the poor showing of Catholics in so many fields, non-Catholics can be forgiven if they sometimes wonder who the real intellectuals might be. This behavior on the part of certain Catholics is a product of the strain under which their own acceptance of Catholic values is placed by the impact of secularized intellectual activity. It is an extreme form of the defensiveness we shall discuss later (Chapter IV, Part 2). Intellectual criticism produces real anxiety for such people, and the result is verbal aggression. Beneath their aggressiveness they are half-consciously aware of the abyss into which criticism and doubt threaten to hurl them.

The foundation of anti-intellectualism is, of course, fear, however it may be disguised by rationalization. Because of his own insecurities and defensiveness the anti-intellectual has very little tolerance for ambiguity and divergence.

Let us face frankly what every sociologist and anthropologist knows from experience. The individual person cannot satisfactorily grasp and securely hold to a working definition of the human situation without taking a tremendous amount on trust from his society and its recognized authorities. Men need some stable definition of life and some stable value system to sustain meaningful effort, yet individual men cannot achieve those things alone. Societies solve such problems by providing cultures, which are the result of accumulated human experience. They contain much of the wisdom, and also much of the nonsense, of the ages. But at any rate they do provide a design for living which enables their members to order the fundamental ambiguity of life, with its problems of impermanence, evil and death.

Christianity has been most sophisticated and most open in its recognition of the nature of this conflict between the human need to know in order to live meaningfully, and the equally real human inability to know the human situation in any final sense. While refusing to derogate reason, it has recognized the inability of natural reason to provide man with an ultimate definition of the human situation.

Christianity offers Divine Revelation exactly at the point where natural reason fails. It supplements the human with the more-than-human in the most transcendent sense, precisely where the total human situation exceeds man's grasp. But this is no cheap and easy solution, for Christianity further holds that the acceptance of the divinely proffered explanation depends upon what it calls faith, understood not as a mere fiduciary reliance upon social or religious or even scientific authority, but as an intellectual assent to what is understood only obscurely—an assent made possible by the action of the Holy Spirit within the believer.

Every cultural attempt to establish a world view—a prerequisite for meaningful human striving—rests ultimately upon accepted opinion. In the case of Christianity (and Judaism) alone a true foundation is offered. Christianity offers the God-given gift of faith. To the social scientist, *qua* social scientist, such faith may appear to be only the natural trust which underlies all cultures and which seems to be the naive expression of an inherent "will to live" and "will to believe" in man, involving a fundamental trust in the universe. Yet reason soon makes men aware that in the case of natural systems of belief, the evidence to justify such trust is inadequate. The deeper level of human concern and human experience and the final dimensions of the human situation are realities which can either be known to man through the gratuitous dispensation of a Higher Power—and then darkly as in the poor looking-glasses of the first century—or not known at all. Christianity offers just such a dispensation. Apart from it the great and impressive structures of society and culture rest upon a void, as the early pagan myths so profoundly suggested. And, as they also intimated, man's life is a dark journey across a bridge thrown by reason and tradition across that void.

The intellectual is the man who, in terms of his advancement of knowledge and his conserving functions with respect to the accumulated knowledge of the past, builds and preserves the bridge over that void. At the same time, in terms of the critical aspects of his role, he is the man who exposes the weaknesses of that very bridge—even showing that parts of it will not really hold us up. From this latter aspect of his role are derived both the suspicion and hostility accorded him by his fellow citizens and the interior anguish he suffers himself.

The relation of natural reason to the human situation is an ambiguous one and cannot but evoke an ambivalent reaction from men. When a society accepts reason, as our Western society did in past centuries, the intellectual with a socially defined role comes into existence. This role then embodies the very ambiguities and ambivalences involved in the basic function of the intellect itself.

The "institutionalization" of reason in our Western civilization is certainly the source of many of our proudest accomplishments. Theology, philosophy, letters, science and technology all reveal its effect. But they also reveal another consequence, the dynamic element which reason— ever acknowledging its own insufficiencies—introduces

into life. Hence the great intellectual conflicts and crises
that have marked our history. For example, consider the
effect of the Copernican revolution upon the Western
mind and on Western man. As John Donne put it:

> And new Philosophy calls all in doubt,
> The Element of fire is quite put out;
> The Sun is lost, and th'earth, and no man's wit
> Can well direct him where to look for it.
> . . . .
> 'Tis all in peeces, all cohaerence gone. . . .

It was in this situation that some Christians, as Lecomte
du Noüy has pointed out, became alarmed, seeing in the
collapse of the old cultural definitions a severe threat to the
faith, which they had too closely identified with these
purely cultural products. The Catholic Galileo found himself in serious trouble with ecclesiastical authority and the
Protestant Kepler was persecuted by the Protestant Faculty
at Tübingen. Luther and Melancthon condemned the
work of Copernicus in scathing terms, even before Catholics had become alarmed by the new developments. Later
the Church forbade Catholics to affirm as fact what Copernicus had stated and Galileo had partially demonstrated
with his telescope.

The real situation was still unclear—neither the Copernican nor the Ptolemaic hypothesis was clearly demon-
strable from evidence. But it is significant that the tendency
of most Christian authorities, Catholic and Protestant, was
either to shy away from the new possibilities or to put
obstacles in the way of new scientific developments. This
was certainly not true of all churchmen—the Jesuits gave
refuge to Kepler when he fled Tübingen—but it was the

case by and large, and the result has been to throw Christianity on the defensive in relation to some of the most important advances of Western man, a position from which we have begun to emerge only in our own time. Such have been some of the historical expressions of this basic tension we are analyzing.

The non-intellectual, if the society in question values learning and knowledge, accords the intellectual the respect commanded by custom. But at the same time he often sees him also as one who attacks—or at least questions—custom and tradition, and who is thereby undermining the bridge that society has thrown over the void. As such, the intellectual cannot but become the object of suspicion and hostility. Even in his conservative function the intellectual may, in his purification of tradition, appear as a destroyer to those who have accepted degenerate versions. Socrates, Aquinas, and Ignatius Loyola were alike regarded as "dangerous" by many of their contemporaries.

The intellectual may be a creative genius like Plato, who discovers a whole new dimension in human existence; he may be a creative critic and synthesizer like Aquinas, who in terms of a vital tradition confronts with courage and intelligence the challenges of new systems of thought and new factual discoveries and thereby leads his culture to new intellectual advances; he may be a great political leader like Pericles, who guides his people through the trials of conflict; he may be a negative though brilliant critic like Abelard who awakens uncertainty, and delights in shocking conservative minds, but at the same time makes solid contributions to the culture of his time; he may, like Galileo, be the innovator who finds himself persecuted in life only to be honored after his death; he may, like Léon Bloy, be a critic who combines acid criticism with iron loyalty to purify and defend tradition; or like Klaus Fuchs he may become lost in the labyrinth into which independent thought has led him, and may thereby betray his society. He may be any one of these, but his character, his problems, and the attitudes of his fellow men toward him are in large part to be explained by the socially structured status which he occupies in society. And in all societies that position will have certain common aspects deriving from the generic nature of the relation between thought and life.

The quest for knowledge involves risk, and risk will always be the object of both admiration and fear, will always evoke acclaim and defense. Moreover, there is the constant temptation to want the solid results of risk without paying the price of risk itself. The status of the intellectual will always reflect these problems, although different societies will evidence them in different ways.

Part 2: The Role of the Specialist: The Structure of Suspicion

Since intellectuals tend to be the ones involved in the advancement of knowledge they also tend to possess special knowledge which is nevertheless of concern to the general run of men. Such specialization may be in areas of human activity that deal with sacred matters, and the specialist may be a "religious specialist."

It is with advances in knowledge which offer obvious advantages to society that the intellectual specialist emerges onto the scene. He may at first be a religious specialist who performs other functions which we should consider scientific—for example, the priestly astronomers of ancient Babylon and Egypt. In societies with a more complex technology there appear specialists whose tasks are chiefly concerned with functions of great importance to the members of the society—the physicist in our own society, for example. Yet these functions remain beyond the competence and even beyond the comprehension of most people. Such tasks demand a period of special training that sets the specialist apart from the layman. The cleric in the Middle Ages, the doctor in the modern world, are in this category.

The result of this special training involving access to specialized knowledge is that to the ambiguities inherent in the intellectual's role are added, in the case of technical specialists, ambiguities derived from the fact that the specialist possesses a monopoly of generally relevant knowledge. When a group has knowledge not available to the majority of men and yet of great significance for their welfare, the non-specialist population is placed in a position of dependence with respect to them. The specialist supplies the needs of the non-specialists, and this may lead to respect or even affection for him on their part. Yet at the same time, dependence can reduce the autonomy of the subject and thereby become a source of frustration; or it may seem to him to detract from his personal worth. In cases where dependence is extremely one-sided and prolonged, it can call forth hostile reactions against the person upon whom the dependence is felt. Such reactions may not be openly antagonistic, but they can be; and even when they are not, the negative element is no less real.

Medical practitioners, for example, are often beset with

such difficulties in the performance of their tasks. The ambiguities involved in the specialist's role are increased in the doctor's case, since he deals with questions of life and death. Such problems arise not only in the relation with the patient but also in connection with the patient's relatives and friends. The doctor may pursue his course of treatment with scrupulous regard for professional ethics, but fears and suspicions are nevertheless aroused in patients and their families, who do not understand the doctor's rationale for his procedure and whose emotional involvement in the case is tremendous.

The resentment of specialists resulting from the ambiguity we have analyzed has been an important element in anti-clericalism as well. For in some societies the relation of the priest to the public has been not unlike that of the doctor in secularized society. In early European society, for example, the priest had not only a special relation to the sacramental means of grace; he was also a member of the only small educated class which had special access to the organs of power and influence. Both factors were productive of suspicion. Here, too, vested interests complicated the picture. But the existence of structured, or "built-in," ambiguity is the point to be noted.

Most intellectuals are specialists of some sort, and hence the problem we have indicated will usually be found to some extent in the relationship between the intellectual and the non-intellectual member of society. A striking example of such a conflict may be seen in the recent controversy between physicists and administrators in connection with the administration and use of atomic energy. It appears that the administrators tend to see the physicists' position as narrowly confined to the "technical" aspects of atomic physics. The physicists, on the other hand, see this attitude as derogating their position in the total prestige structure of modern society.

Moreover, they conceive their position as embodying and symbolizing natural science and its place in man's consciousness and scheme of values. They refuse to see what they consider to be a role of intellectual and cultural eminence—the "noblest of pursuits"—reduced to that of the mere "technician." Like the lawyer who defends legality and his own vested interests simultaneously in defending due process of law, the physicists feel that they are defending the future of society by defending the total status of science, while they resist any infringement of their vested interests as scientists.

Part 3: Activism. The Disvaluation of Pure Knowledge

Another source of ambivalence, or mixed reactions, toward the intellectual on the part of the non-intellectual is to be seen in terms of the dual function of knowledge. Not only is knowledge a value in itself, but it also possesses practical uses. The intellectual is closely identified with the former aspect, although he is often involved in the latter as well. The practical man values the latter aspect—to him the "useful" function—and therefore those identified with it, and regards the former as time-wasting. When the culture of a society emphasizes activism and when the strategic classes are active classes, the value of pure knowl-

edge will have to justify itself in terms of practical potentialities, often as a possible source of "inventions."

In America today, scientists often point to the importance of pure research as the basis for the useful innovations that have developed our technology. There are times
when science is presented as justified almost entirely in
terms of technology and defense. Scientists are often con-
strained to make public concessions to these prejudices
although they themselves value pure knowledge. An amus-
ing example of this is when astronomy appeals for support
in terms of its usefulness to navigation, although it is
doubtful if advances in pure astronomy have helped sailors
much since the time of Ptolemy. Activism tends to belittle
pure knowledge and thereby cast unfavorable reflections
upon the status of the scientist. Hence the scientist is often
caricatured as a crank with a beard and preferably a foreign accent, or, on a lower level, as Mister Peepers, the
bumbling, ineffectual teacher of high school science.

Part 4: The Role of the Intellectual and the Manifest Content of Catholic Culture Patterns

In the present analysis it will prove helpful to introduce
a further set of concepts, a set which perhaps may be a bit
oversimplified as we present them here, but which indicate
a side of social reality of immense importance to any sociological study. An analyst may examine either the *manifest*
or the *latent content* of culture patterns and of status and
role definitions. In other words, since things are not always

to be taken at face value, since they are not always what they seem to be, these two concepts enable us to grasp those things which do not readily meet the observer's eye. By manifest content shall be understood the obvious and palpable content of culture patterns or role definitions. For example, we may say that a college student in this country is expected by his parents, his teachers and even by himself, to devote his major efforts to study in terms of the college curriculum. Yet we all know that there have been cases—more in evidence in the past than at the present time, let us gratefully acknowledge—in which a student who devoted a major portion of his time and energy to study was by common consent branded a "greasy grind" and considered to be an object of contempt. What is important to note is that the second expectation—or role definition—is as much a culture pattern as is the first. It is, of course, inconsistent with the first. How the two fit together in any case becomes an empirical research problem. The second set of expectations are what we mean by the latent content. They exist under the surface. In some cultures it is part of the latent but culturally defined and accepted expectations that soldiers will surrender if the going gets too tough. Thus in China until a few years ago the armies of war lords often changed sides. In our present study it will be important to look at both manifest and latent levels.

We are now ready to state our problem in terms of the sociological concepts we have been considering. The American Catholic group has failed to produce what in the estimation of some of its own intellectual spokesmen, as well as in the estimation of outside observers, friendly, neutral and hostile, would be both qualitatively and quantitatively an appropriate intellectual life. It has failed to evolve in this country a vital intellectual tradition displaying vigor and creativity in proportion to the numerical strength of American Catholics. It has also failed to produce intellectual and other national leaders in numbers appropriate to its size and resources.

The first and most obvious place to look for a possible answer to this problem is the area of culture which we have just designated as its "manifest content," that is, in the manifest content of the culture patterns which are shared by Catholics in the United States. Since the salient and most central of those shared culture patterns are to be found in the doctrines of the Catholic Church, some consideration must be given to these doctrines from the outset.

The dogmas of the Catholic religion are accepted on supernatural faith; but in the act of faith, the intellect is not superseded by grace but supported by it; the intelligibility of the doctrine depends upon the intellectual hold which the believer has on it. Obviously, if the intellectual supports are removed from Catholic life, the institutional structures of the Church must fall back on custom and convention. In an earlier period when Catholic philosophy was, on the natural level, more in harmony with the generally accepted philosophies, these secular philosophies offered another line of defense upon which religious institutions could depend to some extent. Today such secular support no longer exists.

Today the faith which has not been grasped intellectually can be buttressed only by social consensus and an insistence upon conformity to what is generally accepted in Catholic circles. Since the truths of Divine Revelation—the foolishness of the Cross—are by no means readily apparent to a society which seeks after worldly wisdom—or, more vulgarly, requires a sign—intellectual criticism can pose a real threat to an institutionalized Catholicism stripped of its intellectual content.

These obvious facts of our situation must be seen in the larger context of the Church's frequently defensive posture in face of the intellectual movements of modern times. The fact that many of these movements have been frankly agnostic when not irreligious has certainly increased the Catholic tendency toward defensiveness. Thus is the risk of intellectual activity made greater and the tension latent in all intellectual efforts increased.

The first point to be faced—to be faced honestly, frankly and calmly in the spirit of the long Catholic tradition of intellectuality—is the *fact of risk*, which we have seen to be inseparable from intellectual life. Are we engaged in a spiritual quest or in search for a rule of safety? Of course a defensive and constraining policy which inhibits genuine growth will be more costly in the long run. But such a course takes its toll quietly, and those who do not worry about what they do not see find it possible to ignore shocking losses. The "touchy" defensiveness of those who announce the good news of salvation in face of militant secularism is a kind of scandal to thinking men. But it is easier to blame it on the opponent than to re-examine one's own shortcomings.

The risk incurred by intellectual vitality may at times cause clear and dramatic losses. Every intellectually alive period in the Church's history has seen certain extreme developments which became heresies. Yet without these creative periods there would be comparatively little Christian theology and very little developed Christian doctrine. There would, in fact, be very little for even the most conservative-minded of our contemporaries to point to with pride. The fact of risk is based upon our nature as rational animals, and the miseries and the grandeur which characterize our most profound intellectual adventures are inalienable from it. It must be faced squarely.

No one is advocating the removal of pastoral care for the guidance of immature minds or the development of young souls. As a matter of fact I do not believe that the average Catholic today can safely be exposed to the winds of current unbelief without a much better preparation than he has been given—a fact that itself is a comment upon our situation. But Catholic educational leaders must decide whether or not they are willing to promote the development of intellectual maturity. They must decide whether or not they genuinely value the intellect and the intellectual life enough to embark upon a program which might involve the loss of some who are weak in faith and the temporary falling away of others who do not at first encounter meet every crisis of growth successfully. There is no intention here of suggesting concrete policy; we intend merely to indicate the alternatives which must be considered in policy-making.

A vigorous intellectual life would give the Catholic Church a much larger influence in the domestic life of the American Republic and increase the influence of Christian values upon the development of the world situation, now

so fluid and undecided in its basic direction. Even a sec-
tarian vested interest would dictate the wisdom of a bold
Catholic policy in this respect. But it is unlikely that Catholics would decide such matters for ulterior or unworthy
motives. What our enemies often attribute to our evil
intentions is in fact the product of our ignorance. But the
fact is that if we are to remain true to our own basic values
in the new and terrifying situation of today's world we
must decide in favor of intellectual activity and we must
boldly carry out that policy in our operations.

Certainly the present behavior of some Catholics indicates an inadequate response to the challenge of the times.
Anti-intellectualism and the denunciation of "egg-heads";
black and white pronouncements in the fields of opinion
where such pontification is justified neither by faith nor
by science; fear and suspicion of innovation, especially
when it is associated with a secularist source—such reactions are understandable enough in terms of the foregoing analysis.

But the same analysis reveals the complete inadequacy of
these reactions if a realistic meeting of real problems is
what interests us. They are in fact the sociological ana-
logues of neurotic symptoms; they are the expression of
defense mechanisms against facing the uncertainties which
characterize our age. They are not rationally thought-out
judgments and deliberate responses to situations which
have been studied and analyzed by reason. They are, in
short, immature reactions. We use the term immature in
a completely scientific sense to describe reactions which do
not involve the conscious rational evaluation of situations
and issues, but rather derive from unexamined mental

operations conditioned by undigested past experience. The neurotic sees in any authority figure the stern father who tyrannized his childhood. His reaction is an immature one. The person who sees in egg-heads the unrecognized symbol of his own inner uncertainties and who reacts to intellectual questioning and honest differences with dogmatization and abuse, relying entirely on his own peculiar version of "right reason," presents an analogous phenomenon. Father Walter Ong has given as good a definition of maturity as anyone. "Maturity is not achieved," he states, "until a person has the ability to face with some equanimity into the unknown."[2]

We shall discuss later (Chapter IV, Part 1) the martial attitude forced upon American Catholics by their nineteenth-century experience and the related partial segregation of Catholics from American cultural developments. We will note here only that these facts have contributed to creating an atmosphere in which the tensions aroused by the inherent ambiguities of the intellectual role are accentuated. To this defensiveness, we must add in some cases an element of resentment against other groups which have experienced more success. Such an attitude only adds to the original causes for our shortcomings.

There is a kind of vicious circle involved. Our defensiveness inhibits the development of a vigorous intellectual tradition. Our lack of such a tradition keeps our contribution small and leaves us occupying fewer positions of importance in American life than our numbers warrant. This in turn makes us resentful and increases defensiveness, thereby reinforcing the original cause of our difficulties.

We must ask ourselves why some Catholics are afraid of the differences of opinion demanded by a genuine

pluralism. Why is the unusual by that very token sometimes suspect? Is it not that there is a tendency to fear
the very ambiguities which we have analyzed in the previous section? Is it not that conformity and uniformity are
sought as a kind of insurance to create and maintain an
illusion of universality which hides uncertainty? Is it that
we are at times too eager for a comfortable, customary
Catholicism? Is it that in fact our faith does not overcome
the world? that we need sociological props—conformity
and uniformity—to assure us on the natural level that God
is in His heaven, and that in spite of the nasty modern
situation all is really right with the world?

Does our Catholic education form us in the intellectual
virtues, and does it make clear to our intelligent youth that
the risk, and the consequent anxiety, involved in the intellectual life can be an important factor in human growth
to natural and spiritual maturity? Or do we communicate
timidity in face of modern problems, an attitude of nega-
tivism which seeks first the avoidance of danger? Do we
try to convey to young people an understanding of the intellectual's cross—the anguish which is an inevitable part
of his calling—and its human and spiritual significance?
One reads or hears little of such things in Catholic circles
in America, lay or clerical. It is shameful for Catholics to
attack and ridicule secular intellectuals for their confusions
and mistakes when they themselves are perhaps afraid to
face the situations which have confused those intellectuals
and led them into error. Yet such attacks occur. It is a
sense of decency with respect to the frailties of men which
keeps one from giving documentary evidence of such tendencies.

Perhaps our very intellectual weakness makes us fall

prey to what may be called the levelling tendency, the itch to cut intellectuals down to size. Do we tend to deride the egg-heads out of resentment of our own insufficiency? Our dominantly middle-class origins can but increase such levelling tendencies on our part. There are many aspects of these issues which present empirical problems that cannot possibly be answered in an analysis on the present level, but research can provide information to enable us to make a fairer estimate of how widespread the conditions suggested here may be. In fact, that such research has not been undertaken earlier may in itself be an indication of how little value we have placed upon the role of the intellectual and how little we have understood it.

Book Legislation: An Important Example

Arturo Carlo Jemolo in his book on Italian Church-State relations tells how he once, in a discussion with a church dignitary, deplored the lack of Catholic writers in Italy comparable in quality to those produced in France. He commented that the strictness of censorship in Italy created an atmosphere unfavorable to such developments. The ecclesiastic said that he supposed that such must be the case. It evidently never occurred to the churchman that it might be desirable to make any changes in that censorship.

Here in America non-Catholics often see the enthusiasm for censorship that some Catholics display as closely related to the lack of genuine intellectual achievement in Catholic circles generally. As a result they often think of

Catholics as anti-intellectual *en bloc.* This is a kind of
scandal that, although perfectly obvious to those Catholics
who participate in general American intellectual activities
and educational institutions, seems to escape the notice of
many of the more segregated of their co-religionists.

Certainly the connection between such attitudes on the
part of some Catholics and the lack of Catholic creativity
is not quite as close as many non-Catholics suspect, nor do
either of them derive from any necessary anti-intellectualism in Catholic thought. Yet there is a relation involved
here and it deserves some consideration. Perhaps nowhere
in the manifest content of Catholic culture patterns are
elements concerned with the encouragement of cultural
creativity and development of a solid intellectual tradition
so easily accessible to examination as in the *Index Libro-
rum Prohibitorum* and Canon Law with respect to books
as seen in Canons 1384-94 and Canon 1399. It is beyond
the scope of a work of this kind to attempt any detailed
analysis, yet the question is so clearly pertinent to our purposes that some remarks are in order.

The basic fact is that Catholic legislation prohibits the
reading of certain books by name and others by general
categorization. Many of these books are considered necessary for scholarly work in many fields by those competent to make such judgments, and others would appear to
most literate men to be books with which any cultured
person should have at least a passing acquaintance. While
exceptions can be made for good reason, the reasons themselves can burden consciences and moreover such a situation often adds further obstacles to students. When
confronted with these facts by antagonists, Catholic intel-

lectual spokesmen usually point to the fact of these concessions. But this is at times not an entirely candid performance, for such Catholic spokesmen often personally and privately decry the situation that public relations causes them to condone at least to some degree. Of course exceptions are made, in fact have to be made, for otherwise it would be quite impossible to conduct a university or even a good small college. The extent to which they are given, however, varies from institution to institution, and it is difficult to see any general factor that distinguishes one situation from another except the common sense of the various school authorities.

In view of what has been the situation in the past, one can only welcome the recent report that a liberalization of the Church's book legislation is being seriously contemplated.* In what follows I shall simply deal with one fact of my own experience coupled with some observations on the subject made by an English commentator, Monsignor Humphrey Johnson. The purpose of introducing this material is two-fold: first, to indicate from both an American and an English source the type of reaction which seems to have occasioned the "quiet but growing movement" toward a revision of the Church's legislation governing reading and study and second, to point out some of the effects which the present legislation may have had upon the problem being discussed in this study.

I was once asked by an American bishop to address the priests of his diocese on a non-Catholic religious group about which I had done considerable sociological research.

* NCWC news release, appearing in the Catholic press in the weeks of June 16 and June 23, 1958.

Canon 1399 classifies *ipso jure prohibentur* books of writers *haerisim vel schisma propugnantes aut ipsa religionis fundamenta quoque modo evertere nitentes.*[3] Moreover, the same Canon forbids Catholics to read editions of the original text of Sacred Scripture published by non-Catholics in any language whatever. The fact is that had I taken toward this piece of legislation anything at all resembling the attitude that I habitually hold toward the laws of my state and of the United States, I could not have done the study in question. It is true that Canon 1400 allows a Catholic to read non-Catholic versions of the Bible when they do not have heretical introductions or notes. But in my case it was necessary to read the version of Scripture used by the particular group of persons that I was studying.

The conclusion from my own example is quite clear. If I was able to tell the priests anything useful to them in their apostolic work in speaking to them at the request of their bishop, it was because I had not in the previous decade been able fully to interpret the ecclesiastical law the way the usual law-abiding man interprets his relation to legislation and ordinance generally.

Monsignor Johnson here makes a relevant comment. "A canonist may," he writes, "say that this matter admits of a simple solution, that is of reading under the direction of competent ecclesiastical authority. For those studies necessitating only a short excursion into the realm of forbidden literature there will be but little difficulty and this solution may be an easy and admirable one. It will be so especially in the case of the young man who needs to read one or two prohibited books to cram for a degree but afterwards will never open a serious book again. For the really studious the matter is more complex. For permission to read a particular book is of restricted value unless accompanied by a permission to read any other book which may throw light upon that book, in other words a permission to read at the *applicant's discretion,* (italics mine) whether he be an undergraduate or a graduate or not even a university student at all. It is only as he goes along that the scholar learns what he must read."[4]

It is quite clear that the development of the minds of youth is a delicate matter and that it is not wise for everyone to read everything. But the fact seems to be that the youth who generally abide by the laws in this case are those who would be least harmed, while those who will be harmed go ahead and read as they will. The Church certainly has the pastoral duty of guiding the young and the immature. But the Church also needs nothing so much as mature Christians, clerical and lay. One suspects that the present legislation may succeed in partially quarantining Catholics from the kind of knowledge they need to carry out their tasks as Christians in the world. Today, with the great and revolutionary changes that are taking place and with the tremendous challenges and even greater opportunities that are meeting Christians, it is difficult to think that a Catholic body restricted and hedged about by artificial protections can ever achieve the maturity necessary for its role in society.

Lastly, one need hardly point out that, even from the apologetic point of view, it is extremely valuable for the educated Catholic to be able to read "the other side" freely in order to understand it at its best and strongest.

Otherwise, he can scarcely help his fellow-Catholics who may be misled by it, or talk effectively to non-Catholics in their own language. Because so much of the future is involved, it is sincerely and prayerfully to be hoped that Catholic authorities will meet with success as they address themselves to the great problems in this area.

SUMMARY

Today the great problem of the meaning of life is opened up for Western man with almost unprecedented anguish. Christianity's answer can be brought home in such a situation only by a policy of advance, a fact recognized and urged upon us by numerous recent Papal statements on such diverse subjects as the European Union, the United Nations, the lay apostolate, mass communication and disarmament. But the heritage of the old defensiveness remains. It remains in the manifest level of our behavior and in the manifest content of our culture patterns, especially in our book legislation and the unfortunate attitudes it nurtures. Certainly recent progress indicates that a new confidence is being felt by Catholics. Such Catholic confidence in face of the real anxieties that man's situation arouses is based upon faith. With such strength, great advances can be made, but an analysis of our situation indicates that it will require overcoming the real vestiges of the unhappy past of retreat. The security of a social group, as we saw in our earlier analysis, will determine the degree of tolerance it may permit. Our fears and prohibitions often convey to the world the impression that Christians are afraid to face reality as mature men. Only by our fruits can we show such impressions to be false. If our faith has overcome the world, we need fear nothing.

For, in a very real sense, the Catholic has no choice as to whether he shall enter into or remain aloof from the whole range of culture and knowledge. The world is God's handiwork, and, since He has given man the capacities to do it, He must intend man to study it and grow in the dominion of it, to push farther and farther back the horizons of what he can know about the macrocosm and the microcosm, hearing always the voice of Aquinas reminding him that "every truth without exception—and whoever may utter it—is from the Holy Ghost."

CHAPTER III

Reason and Faith

CHAPTER III

Reason and Faith

Since a fundamental tension between the processes of thought and the living of life, between the critical reason and the metaphysical security on which meaningful endeavor depends, may be present below the level of consciousness even in the best adjusted representative of a culture, it was not surprising to find this tension active in the context of Catholic life. Since the Church is, on one level, a human society (and it is only with that level that we are concerned throughout this study), it is inevitable that it should participate in the tensions and ambiguities of the culture in which it lives. Yet the context of Catholic life does add a new element to the general problem. For the Catholic intellectual the tension arises in a specific form, one which is to be found in every period of history and in every country. In our examination of book legislation we saw one of its obvious expressions. We must now pursue the specific Catholic aspects of the question further.

The central question with regard to the Catholic intel-

lectual may be put in this way: Is there, for the Catholic
intellectual, a conflict between reason and faith?

In the nineteenth century the prejudicial notion became
common among scientists that one could not be both a
Christian and a scientist; and certainly a man who was a
scientist of note and a Catholic, like Pasteur, or a scientist
and an orthodox Protestant sectary, like the elder Gosse,
was looked upon as exceptional. Such prejudice (embracing a field much wider than that of physical science) has
by no means disappeared: fed by the poor showing which
Catholics have made in the intellectual sphere generally,
it persists—and in places persists strongly—in our own day.
I myself have had the question put in all seriousness to me
by a highly intelligent and basically fair-minded man:
"How can you be a Catholic and a social scientist?" In
every circle where the ideology of scientism is strong the
Catholic is still widely held suspect.[1]

Such, then, is the simplest and most obvious of hypotheses—that Catholicism and science, and in the present
case Catholicism and the intellectual life generally, are not
"consonant with" one another. In exploring this hypothesis
let us bear in mind a distinction already made. We must
distinguish between the culture patterns which stem
directly from the teachings of the Catholic Church and
the culture patterns derived from other sources, such as
ethnic or national traditions, or the peculiar American
Catholic experience. Our first question then becomes: Are
the explicit teachings of the Catholic Church hostile to the
life of the intellect? Do the teachings of the Catholic
Church militate, therefore, against the development of an
intellectual elite among the American Catholic population?

The first reaction of an American Catholic upon seeing the question stated thus baldly is to utter a resounding NO! Such a reaction is an emphatic personal testimony to our basic Catholic conviction, that the human intellect is of great and positive value, the image of the Divine Intellect, that its pursuit of truth is part of man's genuine fulfillment, and that the intellect will have a central role in the final stage of that fulfillment in the beatific vision.

As a matter of historical record, the Catholic Church has time and time again affirmed with St. Clement of Alexandria, "For 'Thy foot shall not stumble' if thou attribute to Providence all good, whether it belongs to the Greeks or to us. For God is the source of all good things; of some primarily, as of the old and new Testaments; of others by consequence, as of philosophy."[2] Some of her outstanding spokesmen have even been ready to consider with St. Justin that "those who live according to reason are Christians, even though they are accounted atheists. Such were Socrates and Heraclitus among the Greeks, and those like them. . . ."[3] Yet it is just as true, and we must face the fact, that within the Church other tendencies have existed, tendencies which affirmed with Tertullian, "After Christ Jesus we desire no subtle theories, no acute inquiries after the gospel. . . ."[4]

Part I: The Permanent Tension

Ernst Troeltsch in his magnificent sociological analysis of the consequences of the permanent tensions between the Christian ethos and the world affirmed that it was in the realm of the intellect that the Church most easily and most quickly evolved a positive attitude toward the civilization of antiquity.[5] The conviction that truth is one and indivisible, and that reason and revelation cannot at their most profound levels be in contradiction with each other, has remained the dominant characteristic of the Catholic view.

Yet for the social scientist, the hesitations and the ambivalences are also part of the existential picture and as such must be considered and their importance assessed. And the fact is that there were hesitations—understandable and often justifiable hesitations—in the Church's acceptance of the culture of antiquity. Such hesitations indicate that there must have been some ambivalences, some misgivings, some suspicions. Such ambivalences and suspicions indicate further that under certain circumstances a degree of cleavage is possible between Christianity and intellectual activity. The fact that what we might call the "pro-intellectual side" of the ambivalence won out must not obscure the existence of the problem.

Nor was this situation confined to the ancient world. In the early Middle Ages we see dramatized in the striking personalities of St. Bernard and of Peter Abelard the conflict between faith and logic as it took form in the minds of the men of that time. St. Bernard felt that logic when used by men like Abelard was a weapon against the faith and that Abelard's rational curiosity was in fact a kind of blasphemy. "Peter Abelard is trying to make void the merit of Christian faith, when he deems himself able by human reason to comprehend God altogether," exclaimed the great Saint in a letter to Pope Innocent II attacking "this scrutinizer of Majesty and fabricator of heresies."[6] The passage of time has produced a less violent and more just appreciation of Abelard's contribution to the development of Christian philosophy, a contribution to which even the great St. Thomas stands in debt. Of Abelard's temperamental and other difficulties and of the "critical insistency of his nature"[7] we are also aware. But the point of interest here is that the twelfth century like ours reverberated to the conflict between those who felt that they spoke for rational inquiry and those who answered for faith. The fact of the conflict is our chief concern.

We know that the great flowering of learning in the thirteenth century was not unmarked by similar tensions and ambivalences. Aristotle and Averroes were placed under partial ban by popes and bishops, bans which were in university practice honored rather in the breach than in the observance. It surprises the young present-day student of scholastic philosophy to learn that in 1210 and again in 1215, Aristotle's *Natural Philosophy* and his *Metaphysics* were placed under interdict. This ban "was not revoked, but rather provisionally renewed, in 1231, until those works should be properly expurgated." A commission appointed for this task accomplished nothing, and "the old interdict still hung in the air, unrescinded, yet ignored in practice. So Pope Urban referred to it as still effective—which it was not—in 1263. For Aristotle had been more and more thoroughly exploited in the Paris University, and by 1255 the Faculty of Arts formally placed his works on the list of books to be studied and lectured upon."[8]

The career of St. Thomas Aquinas was marked by similar controversy, and he was the object of considerable animosity from those who felt that his exaltation of reason, as they saw it, was dangerous to faith. To many theologians of his day, St. Thomas appeared to be "a dangerous rationalist, infected with the spirit of Averroes, a most unspiritual iconoclast. . . ."[9] St. Bonaventure, one of the greatest of spiritual writers and one certainly not unaffected by the new philosophic spirit, was highly critical of St. Thomas's idea of the role of reason in theology, and in his sermon of 1268, which was in part directed against Thomistic positions, expressed ideas which indicated that "Reason is not to be trusted too much. Faith and mysticism are safer guides."[10] Thomistic propositions were condemned among others in the great "omnibus condemnation" of 1277 on the Continent, and in England a few weeks later.

Of the continental condemnation Etienne Gilson has said that for many theologians it had the effect of "a crucial experiment: i.e. there had been a willingness to trust to philosophy; philosophy meant Aristotle; and now, at last, it was clear where Aristotle and philosophy led a man. . . . After 1277 the whole air of medieval thought is changed. After a short honeymoon, theology and philosophy are thinking that they understand their marriage has been a mistake. While they await the coming divorce—it will not be long delayed—they begin to redivide their property; each claims possession of its own problems and forbids the other to lay a finger on them."[11] St. Thomas was indeed "the one original thinker of the first rank that his age produced," but he faced considerable opposition and, later on, neglect.[12] Intellectual creativity does not come packaged and labelled even in the theological developments of Christian ages.

We are not concerned here with the philosophical issues involved for their own sake. What concerns us is that
the life of the intellect, and in fact the greatest example
of Christian intellectual creativity in the history of medieval philosophy—the synthesis of Aristotelian science with
Catholic faith culminating in the work of St. Thomas—
was marked throughout by conflict. The innovator was at-
tacked by more conservative thinkers, his orthodoxy was
suspect, and he was even condemned by agencies of institutionalized authority. His later acceptance—and even his
acceptance by the Pope in his own lifetime—must not
blind us to St. Thomas's difficulties. There were many who
felt that faith did not sit easily with St. Thomas's brand
of reason. The basic ambivalences of which we spoke
earlier remained, and they remained important. It is perfectly true that in the end Catholicism always decided in
favor of the human intellect and its rightful role in man's
destiny, but the decision each time was marked by hesitation and by conflict.

Again in the Renaissance, a period marked by what Pope
Leo XIII considered a deplorable spirit of innovation,
when men sought a religious world view which would affirm the goodness of life in the world, and the value of
reason and of beauty, Christians showed themselves divided in face of the new challenge. Yet as a whole the
movement was encouraged by popes and prelates, who indeed at times went further in encouraging novelties than
would seem wise to the soberer afterthought of later generations.

In what is almost our own day, despite scientific and
atheistic ideologies, the Catholic Church has continually

affirmed its conviction that there could be no real contradiction between the Christian religion with its deposit of revealed truth on the one hand, and the valid findings of the new sciences on the other. And indeed at the present time, which has witnessed a development of new obscurantisms and systematic pessimisms, the Catholic Church has displayed itself as a veritable champion of rational thought and has time and again affirmed its confidence in the human intellect.

Yet against this positive record we must also record the fact that Christianity has often been found alienated from, and even in opposition to, the development of modern science. Certainly this is not to be explained in terms of a stubborn Christian obscurantism, as anti-Christians have charged. It was due to socially conditioned, concrete situations, which must be carefully analyzed to be understood. But the fact is that such regrettable historical "accidents" as the blanket rejection by many churchmen of Galileo, Darwin, Lyell and Einstein were possible because there were deep ambivalences characterizing the relations between faith and reason as these relations were experienced in their historical reality in the lives of fallen mankind.

Lecomte du Noüy, who can hardly be called a hostile critic, has stated that when the Church encountered "individuals who dared to think independently in certain fields, it often looked on them with a suspicious eye. When, furthermore, these individuals were geometers and asserted, in contradiction to current beliefs, that the world turned around the sun, they became not only suspect but dangerous. . . ."

He continued, "This was an error. At a period when a

reawakening of human curiosity, soon to flower into the
scientific spirit, could be observed on all sides, this intransi-
gent attitude was shortsighted. It alienated a goodly number of the very people the Church should have called to
her bosom. The clergy should have understood that all attacks on freedom of thought, when neither morals nor
dogma were concerned, made enemies of the very people
it most needed. The Church became frightened; it
doubted."[13]

Some may object that such statements as this one by a
profoundly religious scientist are one-sided. Others may
assume a defensive position and remind us that *De Revolu-
tionibus Orbium* was dedicated by Copernicus to the Pope.
But all statements are one-sided, or at least they cannot be
all-sided. Lecomte du Noüy's interpretation deserves serious consideration, for his basic interpretation is quite in
accordance with the facts of the historical situation. The
fact is that Christianity and science did become alienated
from each other. The Church had good reason to suspect
many of the ideas current at the time, but the manner of
meeting them, seen in retrospect, was on the whole quite
ineffective. A noted historian of science has stated that
the scepticism of the seventeenth century "was encouraged
by the obstructive attitude of the Roman Catholic clergy
in France, who helped to strengthen the impression that
the Church was the enemy of scientific discovery and,
indeed, of anything new."[14]

It is undeniable that modern science in its development
in astronomy, geology and anthropology found itself in
crucial respects in a state of tension and even of conflict
with the Christian religion and with the Catholic Church.

It is a fact that is dogmatized and endlessly repeated in the ideologies of scientism. But some ground for such mythologies does indeed exist in the historical record. The "crime of Galileo" remains the great symbol of that grand scandal—in the literal sense of *skandalon*—the "Dreyfus Case" of the scientific tradition, an incident which, to paraphrase Père Congar, churchmen can never ponder too much. That they have often not pondered it quite enough is evidenced by the fact that the works of Galileo remained on the *Index* until the middle of the nineteenth century.[15]

It is not our task here to explore the historical and sociological problems involved in what we have just been discussing, although they cry for the attention of Catholic scholars and social scientists. All we are trying to do here is to suggest the kind of documentation that is easily available in offering *prima facie* evidence to show that Catholic thought has experienced ambivalence, hesitation and conflict in relation to scientific development. Catholic thinking accepted the intellectual life, but the concrete forms of that acceptance in all periods reveal certain significant ambivalences. The demonstration of formal harmonies, though indicative of a deeper area of agreement, can sometimes serve only to obscure the real historical difficulties, which indicate that there seems to be a certain permanent tension—a perennial strain—between the Christian faith and its demands, on the one hand, and the requirements of the intellectual life, on the other—or, to use more conventional terms, between faith and reason.

The tension may in certain situations be the source of great intellectual creativity, as in the case of St. Thomas, in whom it issued to the advantage of both faith and reason; or it may in other circumstances result in the kind of serious alienation seen in the Galileo case. It may deepen faith or it may frustrate creativity; it may also lead to heresy and unbelief. The existence of the tension throughout Christian history is the first important finding to be registered for our present purposes.

Part 2: The Abiding Temptation

Unlike some traditions of Western thought, Catholic teachings do not make the intellectual life the supreme good. The spiritual life is open to all from the simplest soul to the genius. Thus the intellectual values accepted and emphasized by Catholicism are always in some sense secondary to deeper—though not anti-intellectual—orientations of man toward God, a total openness to God and His grace and a complete incorporation into the Mystical Body of Christ through the sacraments and, where the liturgical life is developed and valued, through the public prayer of the Church.

This subordination of the intellectual life to a larger Christian context can in fact become an important safeguard for and guarantee of the welfare of the intellectual life itself. Catholic spirituality and direction toward the spiritual life, when deep and genuine, can prevent the divorce of intellectual pursuits from community life, especially if a genuine Catholic community life has developed around the liturgy. But the subordination of intellectual values within the general religious context can also be interpreted by certain Christian spokesmen as a derogation of intellectual activity generally.

Which of these two interpretations of the Catholic position and its implications is given is not unrelated to the background and social situations of those who interpret, and also of those who accept the interpretation. The clergy are in general those who teach as well as the members of certain religious orders who administer the parochial school systems. What kind of interpretation of the subordination of intellectual values do these groups give? Monsignor Ellis suggested, as we noted above, that perhaps some of our schools were seeing their role in terms of moral formation alone, to the exclusion of proper emphasis upon intellectual development. How widespread is such a condition? Certainly the background of teachers and administrators plays an important part in this respect, for the way one interprets the Catholic position in concrete cases will be influenced by one's own cultural background. From what social classes and what regions of the country are our personnel drawn, and how does this influence their interpretation? Certainly we know that, generally, lower-middle-class groups do not recognize the importance of intellectual things and are quite likely to see the Catholic subordination of the intellectual values as an "official" disparagement of those values. They thereby read into Catholic attitudes the perspectives of their own social backgrounds.

How does seminary education affect the kind of interpretation that is given? How do priestly duties and the kinds of social relationships which they involve with the laity affect the interpretation? Certainly in these areas may be found some of the causes of why we so often think that the practical things come first and that learning may be left to follow by itself as best it can.

Some of the answers we seek will be found in the area of latent content, which we shall consider below (Chapter V). Others may be found in explicit statements on the teaching and preaching level. Some time ago, for example, a metropolitan newspaper reported that a Catholic preacher delivered a sermon to a military congregation on the evils of intellectual pride. With all the moral problems involved in modern war, it seemed a strange choice.

It suffices for our purposes to note that in the Catholic scheme of values, the intellectual life may receive insufficient emphasis if its subordination to the total spiritual development of man is misunderstood. One of the concrete forms that this disvaluation may take is seen in the assumption that because we are Catholics and have the deposit of faith there is really no need for intellectual inquiry. Intellectual inquiry, in this view, is quite unnecessary except for practical purposes, for so far as what the Greeks called *theoria*—intellectual answers to the problems of man—is concerned, we Catholics already have all the answers.

The Catholic tradition then becomes understood as a manual of formulae to be memorized and applied. Verbalism replaces genuine ontological confrontation; and quest is replaced by a kind of intellectual suspended animation. Practical things—conceived of as religiously "neutral"—tend to take up the time not spent in religious devotions.

Catholic research must be concerned with these important questions, for if the concrete expression of Catholic teaching tends to stifle a spirit of inquiry, if it tends to divorce the intellectual quest from the central meaning of Christian life, then its influence on the formation of young minds will more than offset the positive evaluation of the intellect given in explicit Catholic doctrine. Closely connected with this is the question, What does Christian formation in the intellectual virtues mean? Certainly it involves an appreciation of the point made by A. N. Whitehead, "The worship of God is not a rule of safety—it is an adventure of the spirit. . . ."[16] Is this in fact the spirit we have fostered? It is important to determine whether our difficulties do actually begin at this point. It is one thing if the latent influences of culture and of social structure modify and frustrate the positive attitudes given by our manifest teaching. It is quite another if the teaching itself is so presented that it belittles the intellectual quest and the pursuit of knowledge in the first place. Catholic thought contains tensions that in practice make such developments possible. How common they are is an empirical question deserving serious research.

Many teachers of religion in Catholic institutions are increasingly aware of these problems, and have been willing to attempt changes in face of them.* A dissertation submitted to The Catholic University in 1951 was a study of forty-two colleges in what the investigator chose as a representative cross-section of one hundred twelve Cath-

* One of the most encouraging recent developments within American Catholicism is The Sister Formation Movement, as notable for the enthusiastic support it has engendered as for its far-seeing direction.

olic colleges for women in the United States; it showed very few departments "drifting along satisfied" with old methods and procedures.[17] The author found, however, that "In coming abreast of contemporary demands, religious teaching lags in some respects."[18] Among the factors hindering an adequate response to the present challenge facing the Christian life, the author found three items of particular interest to us here. The first is a failure even to realize the import of that challenge. Moreover, the study states that: "Out of the ten colleges that seem to manifest the most vigorous response to the challenge, only two are in the East."[19]

Two other factors deserve consideration: "(1) retention of the negative approach in moral instruction; (2) a tendency to inculcate an over-individualistic spirituality.[20] The relation of both to defensiveness in face of secularization and the partial segregation of Catholicism from important areas of the national culture suggests itself immediately and also deserves study. Are Catholics being influenced by their own institutions of learning to withdraw in a defensive posture in face of the modern American world? The tendency to inculcate an over-individualistic spirituality, overstressing the personal as against the social, "seems to persist," despite "evidence that much progress has been made" in this respect. Such spiritual "isolationism" certainly increases the tendency to segregation which our peculiar history has forced upon us, although ironically enough it is in large part derived from the excessive individualism and the loss of the sense of the Mystical Body which have characterized so much Catholic spirituality in modern times, and is in part a subtle effect of secularization upon us. Certainly all these three factors militate against introducing the younger generation to modern man's adventure in the quest for knowledge, with resulting maturity, and as such have a deleterious effect upon the development of the intellectual life among American Catholics.

Another dissertation submitted at the same university in 1952 studied the condition of religious instruction in a large sample that represented nearly fifty percent of Catholic men's and co-educational colleges and universities in the United States. Here too we see awareness of the problem and the need to get away from those conditions which make for what one respondent called "the increasing religious formalism we see among our graduates and students,"[21] although in many cases the problems did not seem to be realized in their full dimensions.[22] For example, in answer to the question: "In view of recent theological developments, papal pronouncements, etc., on social and socio-religious problems, do you feel that the Religion curriculum needs to be rethought and reoriented?" Forty department heads answered this question, and 29, or 73 percent of them, either answered affirmatively or showed favorable interest. Yet nine department heads answered in the negative, while two stated that the idea was so new to them that they did not want to make a statement about it.

This study took up the important question of the effects of an arid intellectualism in the teaching of religion. Respondents who had thought seriously about the problem made interesting observations, offered and summarized by the author. It was felt, for example, that "we tend to educate minds not men."[23] On this point several respondents suggested that "the present procedure, while theoretically directed toward informing the intellect, in too many cases reduces itself to demanding the memorization of systematized formulae, which the student relays minutely to examination papers, in order to obtain passing grades. This procedure seems to be a factor contributing to the increased formalism of religious practice so commonly observable today. Of itself, such instruction produces neither understanding, appreciation, nor motivation for Christian living." The author continues: "The pedagogical system itself is not in keeping with the vitalizing nature of the subject. It tends, rather, to devitalize dynamic doctrine. . . ."[24]

The religion teacher alive to his problem is concerned with these difficulties because they cause him to fail genuinely to communicate religious knowledge in such a way that it becomes part of the student's very being. In this, of course, he is perfectly right, for that should be his chief concern. Our own interest here is in the kind of intellectual attitudes it fosters. Religion is an ultimate thing embracing the many-sided reality of man's life and aspirations. It is a matter of the whole man and, as Catholic tradition has always insisted, is not simply a matter of the "emotions," but of cognition as well.

If we fail to engage our students in such a central intellectual quest as religion, how can they develop a genuinely open intellectual attitude toward other fields of knowledge? Is it a great wonder that the orientation to college as merely a means to social and economic mobility—an orientation that their social class backgrounds incline them toward anyway, in too many cases—is perpetuated? In our failure to develop the intellectual life, we must not smugly assume that it is because we sought first the kingdom of God that all these things have been denied to us. We have rather failed to vitalize instruction, to use Father Simonitsch's significant term. If we make the most vital of subjects lacking in vitality, what are we doing to young minds?*

This brings us to a question concerning which fewer empirical data are available. But it is necessary to ask to what extent the methods used in the seminaries for training secular priests are the same as those used in enclosed religious communities. One suspects that in some cases there is a kind of cleavage between the search for perfection and the intellectual quest. St. Thomas places the intellect in the center of the whole man's aspiration toward God. If intellectual activity becomes identified with quasi-Cartesian logic-chopping and sheer rote memorization, St. Thomas's thesis is in fact being overthrown. Further, it must be asked, do many religious look upon study only as a kind of ascetic discipline of the will—as work in the most penitential sense—placing insufficient emphasis on the role of the intellect in the spiritual growth to perfection? Is professional work put squarely in the center of the vocation? If not, basic Catholic values are not being transmitted. These questions must be asked, for there is evidence in American Catholic life which suggests that in some cases they must be answered in the negative.

There are two aspects of seminary education that seem to deserve special attention. First of all is the almost com-

* In the light of questions such as these one can only welcome gratefully the recent establishment of the Confraternity of Teachers of Sacred Doctrine in Catholic Colleges, which represents a truly professional approach to the problems raised in this area.

plete segregation of the seminary and the seminarian from the educational life of the community as a whole. This extreme isolation grew out of Tridentine reforms intended to meet real difficulties of the Reformation period, but it preserves a kind of artificial element in the relationship between the priest and the secular world. Moreover, it cannot but widen immensely the gap that the partial segregation of the American Catholic experience has created between Catholicism in America and much of the intellectual activity of the country. Secondly, the attitude cultivated in the seminarian appears at times to be characterized to a high degree by a kind of passive receptivity; the impression is given that Christian learning is something "finished," and that education is a formation to be accepted from established authority with a minimum of individual initiative and critical activity on the part of the student. The attitudes of the priest have an especially strategic influence on Catholic attitudes generally. For that reason seminary education deserves close attention as a possible source of many of the attitudes which are at the present time inhibiting creative intellectual development among Catholics.

It is quite clear to almost every dean of a Catholic university in this country that religious superiors do not always understand the role of the intellectual life even when they themselves are trying to conduct institutions of learning. They often choose people for professional tasks without a proper regard for the natural talents and inclination of the person. Then work becomes a long penance, and quite apart from its effect upon spirituality—and certainly St. Thomas's teachings would make one very suspicious of its results in that sphere—it will never create genuine intellectual creativity or even teaching efficiency. In acting in this way superiors defeat their own ends and aims, and moreover, they place a useless and actually unjust burden upon the duty of obedience, or at least exploit the loyalty and idealism of the young priest or nun. There is no telling how widespread such practices are, but they do exist and are sufficiently frequent to be a practical problem in Catholic education today.

The fact that some religious superiors do not understand the demands of intellectual life in America today can further be deduced from what is too often their attitude toward the lay faculty.* Substantial salaries are important not because lay teachers are motivated by "materialism" but because money is needed for the support and education of families; because furthermore in our society money is not important only for its own sake but as a symbol of worth, a testimony to the status and prestige of the occupation involved. Not only the individual teacher, but the profession is demeaned when a city pays its school janitors as much as, or more than, its school teachers.

In addition to the salary factor, there is for both religious and lay faculty the problem of the teaching load. Often it is said in extenuation of the fact that every member of the faculty is carrying far too heavy a burden of teaching hours that facilities have to be expanded; that financial difficulties thus will not permit the expansion of the faculty. The result is that the quality of the teaching inevitably suffers; the potentialities for scholarship among gifted students

* For an extremely interesting study of this point, one might consult the article of Professor John Kane in *Ave Maria* (November 16, 1957) and the more general remarks of Oscar Perlmutter in *The Commonweal* (April 11, 1958), together with the correspondence called forth (May 9, 1958).

and members of the faculty, lay and religious, cannot be developed. Yet the impression is unavoidable that some communities are willing to let these conditions exist indefinitely. But would it not be far better to house the institution in temporary quarters while the funds available were devoted to what are the real first necessities of education? Is this emphasis on physical facilities wholly free of the element of materialism?

If a family in the world were thus to dispose its budget, with the emphasis on physical facilities, religious would be quick to detect the unbalance. Yet for the religious community no less than for the family in the world the distribution of the budget is a clear indication of the values which are held to be really important.

All this is, of course, complicated by the fact that very often persons in religion have not a very realistic appreciation of the problems of the laity in the concrete setting of mid-twentieth-century America.

The arid intellectualism of which we have found more than mere traces and the negative defensive approach on moral questions suggest that we may have a restricting effect on many of our students, both clerical and lay. If that is the case, we may be teaching religion but we are not teaching the Catholic religion. Let us simply recall St. Paul's warning concerning the letter and the spirit. Moreover, it suggests that we are at times in danger of making the worship of God, in A. N. Whitehead's phrase, a rule of safety, instead of a call to the fulfillment of human nature and its elevation to communion with the higher realm of the Divine Being.

SUMMARY

We have seen in this chapter that the tension between faith and reason has resulted throughout history in a tension between Catholicism and the intellectual quest; that this tension can have positive or negative effects in both spheres, depending upon the concrete circumstances of the case; and that in spite of the continuous Catholic tradition of intellectuality, it has resulted in scandalous situations in the past. Moreover, we have seen that the manifest content of Catholic teachings is open to serious misinterpretation in a manner that militates against genuine intellectual development. Moreover, persons from certain status backgrounds in society—lower-class and lower-middle class—may be inclined by their social conditioning to just such misinterpretation. Finally, we have considered the actual methods of transmitting the manifest content of Catholic teachings, to see what factors in that area have a bearing on the situation. We shall now explore these problems further in the next two chapters.

CHAPTER IV

The American Catholic Heritage

Part 1: The Divided Man

Part 2: Catholic Defensiveness

CHAPTER IV

The American Catholic
Heritage

So far in our analysis two elementary points have been made, and they provide the basis for the whole of our future discussion. First, the relation of reason to life is characterized by a fundamental ambiguity, and this ambiguity will be reflected in the role of the intellectual in any society which accords reason a place among its central values. Secondly, because of its altogether unique solution to that fundamental ambiguity and its defense at the same time of the role of reason, the basic tension between thought and living will, for Christianity, often take the form of a tension between reason and faith. Yet, vital though these two starting points are for our analysis, it is not sufficient to see these major aspects of the problem in the abstract. Consideration must also be given to their concrete manifestations in the context of American Catholic history. All that we have already said has implied that past experiences have an important effect in conditioning present actions. Hence it is necessary at this point to examine some of the salient aspects of our past which bear directly on our present concerns. We cannot hope to do anything like justice to this immense and important topic, but we can at least indicate the broader lines of influence which are involved.

Let us proceed directly to the basic historical problem. It must be recognized that in the task of developing a native intellectual tradition the Catholic community in this country has been faced with two problems, whereas for our fellow citizens of Protestant background there has been but one. Both they and we have had to relate the basic ideas and values of our respective heritages to the unfolding events of the American adventure. But we have had, in addition, the difficulties arising from the fact that we have been a minority group endeavoring to relate our distinct religious and cultural traditions to the changing patterns of a dominant non-Catholic culture. Under any conditions the difficulties which faced us would have been twice as great as those which faced the Protestant majority. But the fact that we were for so long an immigrant group, or a group not far removed from immigrant status, and were consequently to such a great extent the hewers of wood and the drawers of water, made the problem still more acute. These conditions caused us to remain much longer than might otherwise have been the case in a state of intellectual dependency upon the Catholic culture of Europe, from which we were moreover cut off to some extent, owing to our economic circumstances.

Although Catholics were not at first well received in this

country, and our history is marked by the intolerance and prejudice which we met upon arrival on these shores, the assimilation of the successive streams of Catholic immigration was nevertheless genuine. Catholics came to consider themselves true Americans, and eventually to be accepted as such by the majority of their non-Catholic neighbors. Yet in a real sense we differed from the immigrants of other religious backgrounds in our ability to assimilate ourselves to American culture in the various realms of social life. In the political and economic spheres, Catholics, like the descendants of other immigrants, came to participate wholeheartedly in the common life of America. Loyalty to American institutions and identification with them became deeply imbedded in the American Catholic consciousness.

But in the intellectual sphere, in the area of values and ideas, the Catholics had to stand somewhat apart from the general run of their fellows; the distinct character of the Catholic cultural heritage had the effect of preventing the Catholic community from participating fully in the general American developments. Much of American intellectual history represents the transformation of Protestantism— especially of Calvinism—under the impact of American conditions and liberal ideas derived from the eighteenth-century European Enlightenment. Typical of the processes involved are: the revivalism of the eighteenth and nineteenth centuries; the long-term revolt of American Protestants against Calvinist pessimism, culminating in the recognition of the freedom of the will and the efficacy of human action; and the intensive secularization of American culture during the second half of the nineteenth century. All these processes started from the older Protestant positions, and all represented great collective experiences of the American Protestant population. While these transformations were taking place, Catholics were generally engaged in the basic processes of assimilation to the new society and its culture. Their separate heritage as well as their specific contemporary problems served to detach them from these processes. But while it was in the nature of the case that the Catholic community could not participate directly in these developments, it could not avoid experiencing their effects.

Part 1: The Divided Man

One result of this experience—one that deserves very careful analysis and evaluation by Catholic writers—has been our simultaneous incorporation into and alienation from American culture. Our minds are in a sense compartmentalized in relation to American society as a whole. On the one hand we have formed a firm identification with certain aspects of the national culture—notably in the fields of politics, constitutional law and economics. On the other, we have developed in certain areas an aloofness amounting at times to alienation. This is especially true with respect to the development of native thought in spheres involving basic world views and values, where our past has made homogeneity with the Protestant-derived tradition difficult or even impossible.

This subtle marginality of ours has been the cause of inner conflict as well as of external difficulties. It has resulted in a subtle division of the American Catholic mind. On the one side is a firm identification with American society and strong loyalty to and love for its basic institutions. On the other is an alienation from the intellectual and spiritual experiences which, as we have seen, were central for those of Protestant background. Sometimes this cleavage manifests itself in a superficial over-identification with everything American—an over-identification which disguises a profound alienation. Our past difficulties increase our present tendency toward such over-identification.

It is this problem, almost more than the more obvious reasons, which justifies the existence of Catholic institutions of higher learning in this country. An institutional context is necessary for the correlation of the Catholic- and Protestant-derived elements of the continuous American tradition if the dilemma arising from our history is to be resolved. Moreover, in serving the Catholic community of America by performing this function, the Catholic university is also of service to the American culture in general, for it thus provides another voice in the great cultural exchange without which national intellectual development might be deprived of a whole range of contributions.

It cannot be repeated too often, to cite but one example, that in part the role of the Catholic intellectual in America must be "prophetic"—endlessly championing points of view which are counter to those prevailing in his society. Divorce is now part of the American way of life; euthanasia may become so. The Catholic intellect, rightly used in the secular order, not only can profit by the positive results of the best modern thinking but can also serve to correct some of its unfortunate elements, but only on condition that Catholic thinkers be regarded as collaborators and not as deadly enemies.

Hence it is necessary first that a genuinely creative intellectual tradition should be developed among American Catholics. At the present time, unfortunately, the means taken to resolve this inner conflict—one from which no literate Catholic can be wholly immune—are often inappropriate. For some Catholics this division and compartmentalization has resulted in an overanxious desire to identify themselves with America in those areas where their history has made such identification possible, and to proclaim these areas of life, and the views derived from them, as the very essence, the "badge" of true "Americanism." Such people tend to see certain liberal ideas and ideals—in fact quite genuinely American in origin and descent although different from, and at times in opposition to, Catholic values—as "unAmerican," and to join in strictly partisan conflicts to exorcise them. There are indeed those for whom the whole Enlightenment tradition, long since transplanted and developed in its American setting, becomes a subversive foreign import of the latter days. Such behavior tends merely to increase and make more rigid the Catholic alienation and to make a positive solution to the underlying problem much more difficult.

Part 2: Catholic Defensiveness

To this major structure of our problem must be added another dimension, already alluded to above and to be discussed in further detail below. The fact is that Catholicism has been thrown on the defensive by the secularization of culture which has marked the last four centuries of European and American development. These centuries have seen until quite recently a steady retreat—a defensive rearguard action—on our part (and in fact on the part of all believing Christians) before an advancing, and at times a militant, secularism.

A little less than a hundred years ago, educated non-Catholics considered that the Catholic Church had been vanquished, and many had written it off as defunct. "Popery can build new chapels," said Carlyle a little over a century ago; "welcome to do so, to all lengths. Popery cannot come back any more than paganism can—which still also lingers in some countries. But, indeed, it is with these things as with the ebbing of the sea: for minutes you cannot tell how it is going; look in half an hour where it is—look in half a century where your popehood is!"[1] Carlyle has proved to be a bad prophet, but the extremities to which the Church was reduced in the mid-nineteenth century were real enough. As Paul Tillich said twenty years ago: "Since the Counter-Reformation Catholicism has been fighting a defensive war directed equally against Protestantism on the one hand and autonomous civilization on the other."[2] By "autonomous civilization" Tillich refers to a self-sufficient secularism.

This defensiveness affected many aspects of the Catholic outlook and militated against a more flexible engagement with the modern world. But it was primarily a defensiveness dictated by harsh necessity and not one deriving from any basic rigidity of the Catholic faith in terms of meeting new situations and diverse cultures. Moreover, it was a defensiveness which, however heavy the cost—and the cost was heavy—accomplished its object. It has preserved the deposit of faith and remained true to the Church's divine commission.

For the last several decades in Europe there has been evidence that the state of siege has passed. A new flowering of Catholic thought and culture seems imminent and has indeed already come. A period of cultural advance appears to be opening up for the ancient Catholic tradition. In fact, Catholicism today stands foremost in the defense of the whole of European civilization, while it reaches out creatively to meet new problems and to bring its eternally new message to the continents struggling for maturity.

But this state of siege of the Universal Church in the last century deprived American Catholics, pioneering in the new country, of the stimulus they might otherwise have received from their European brethren. Had the present Catholic renaissance come earlier in France, perhaps the intellectuals of that country might have given more significant aid, instead of at times almost interpreting our national attitudes as a new heresy. Yet in America the Church accomplished basic tasks under conditions often difficult and trying. The Americanization of the immigrant, the building of churches and of schools, the development of colleges and universities, and the contribution of able men, lay and clerical, to American life bear testimony to this. We have not done as well in some of these respects as we should have, but even here the judgment is our own, and our present discussion of these problems, to which this book is but one modest contribution, bears testimony to our growing ability for mature self-criticism. It is on the basis of the accomplishments of the past that the present discussion is possible, and it is those very accomplishments which give us so many reasons to anticipate its success.*

Within this larger historical context we must now examine some of the more detailed processes of our historical experience and their effects upon us. A number of works by Catholic writers in America have dealt with the various aspects of these problems, and from these we shall try to extract the elements most pertinent to the present problem. Catholic writers have generally ascribed the lack of a vital intellectual tradition among American Catholics to a cluster of past difficulties and their present derivatives which can be summarized under six heads.**

1. The lack of a Catholic intellectual heritage in this country related both to the lower-class origins and the present dominantly lower- and lower-middle-class composition of the American Catholic population.

2. The lack of scholarly motivation among American Catholics related to such lower social positions and origins on the one hand, and, on the other, to the expectation that the priests will do the scholarly work while the laity concentrate on other things.

3. The inferior economic position of Catholic groups.

4. The difficulties involved in the process of as-

* For an interesting discussion of some of these accomplishments in the last century see Robert D. Cross, *The Emergence of Liberal Catholicism in America* (Cambridge, Harvard University Press, 1958).

** This summary is drawn from the works of Monsignor John Tracy Ellis, John J. Kane, Theodore Maynard, George N. Shuster and the contributors to the Putz and Ward volumes, most of which are cited in place in this book.

similating millions of immigrants and the problems related to immigrant and post-immigrant status.

5. The defensive, martial and even ghetto mentality brought about by partial alienation and the specific minority experience of American Catholics.

6. Prejudice, hostility and discrimination.

To the difficulties inevitable for a Catholic community adjusting itself to a dominantly non-Catholic culture, which we have already described, must be added the positive disabilities imposed upon Catholics, the intolerance with which they were often treated and the problems of immigration and assimilation. All these factors have tended to segregate the American Catholic population, to hinder the participation of Catholics in the national life, and to make the development of a creative relationship between Catholicism and the national culture more complicated and difficult. These difficulties no longer exist in quite the same form as they once did but they have not passed away. Rather they live on in the attitudes of voluntary segregation and defensiveness which form part of the present American Catholic outlook and erect intangible barriers across the path of our progress.

Moreover, there has developed a considerable lack of awareness among American Catholics, laity and clergy alike, as to the degree to which such attitudes are not the result of our free choices, intellectually considered and rationally concluded, but are merely an automatic response produced by an earlier process of social conditioning. The widespread persistence of such attitudes and their inaccessibility to rational analysis and criticism constitutes an important aspect of our problem and will be the object of later consideration.

It is most important that the six factors we have listed should not be understood simply as elements of the past which time alone will cause to disappear. The writers who have suggested them have not put them forward as excuses, but rather as contributions to a diagnosis of the contemporary situation. That these disabilities are far from correcting themselves with the passage of time but instead remain entrenched in our present-day psychology is suggested by a number of further considerations. Our defensiveness, for example, forced upon us as it has been by circumstances, is a *present barrier* and not merely a remnant of our past. The fact is that although Catholics elsewhere—and not Catholics alone but all believing Christians—have been placed on the defensive by the alienation of the Christian spirit from the modern world, they have produced important intellectual contributions. Yet in America, a country that ranks third among the nations of the world in Catholic population and first in Catholic financial assets, the problem of the lack of an adequate intellectual development has been most acute in its manifestations. That is to say that while the American problem is indeed a part of a worldwide problem—the loss of Catholic initiative over a whole range of vital intellectual fields—it is a much more severe and serious variation of it, complicated by native American Catholic elements.

Sometimes attempts are made to explain the present situation by putting the blame, as it were, on the specifically American quality of American Catholics and of American Catholic life. America as a whole, so this argument runs, has preferred action to thought. It has tended to play down and belittle things of the mind.

There is no denying that this characterization contains an element of truth and that American life has from the beginning placed a premium upon action. But there is another side to the picture. America's early desire to produce an educated Protestant clergy gave rise to great universities on the east coast—Harvard, Princeton and Yale—which have produced Presidents, statesmen, scientists and thinkers in no small numbers. Around them a host of other institutions of learning grew up, each producing men of genuine capacity. The history of American thought, of American science, of American literature and of American art in the brief 182 years since the colonies won their independence shows clearly that thinking has been an American vocation. The American developments and experiments in education, the pioneer foundation of schools and the establishment of land-grant colleges—in short, the whole American past—proves that in spite of her orientation towards practical activity, America has both produced and honored men of considerable intellectual stature, as the range of names from Jefferson through Peirce, Mann, Dewey and our growing list of Nobel Prize winners attests.[3]

This attempt to place the responsibility for our difficulties upon the supposedly unintellectual nature of our national life may appeal to some European intellectuals who, uninformed about America and American things, repeat stereotypes of their own concoction in order to find a scapegoat for their present native frustrations and aggressions; but no American, Protestant or Catholic, can take it quite seriously. In fact the European myth of America's "materialism" collapses with a very cursory examination of the realities, and today few informed Europeans would give it much attention.

Intolerance is, however, another matter, for the reality of such intolerance in the past and even its subtle persistence in some forms in the present cannot be denied. But here matters have certainly improved in terms of the objective American situation. Moreover, we must not make the easy assumption that the experience of intolerance is incompatible with intellectual growth and development, for were this the case how could one possibly explain the tremendous intellectual development shown by American Jewry?

Poverty has certainly been an important factor, but here comparison with this same group gives food for thought. It is doubtful if even the Irish immigrants, perhaps the poorest of the nineteenth-century arrivals to these shores, were much poorer than the eastern European and Russian Jews who came after 1890, except possibly in the worst years of the Irish potato failure of the 1840's. Yet these eastern European Jews would, upon an empirical count, be found to have contributed a larger proportion of their children and grandchildren to academic and scholarly life than have Catholic immigrants as a whole.

It may be seriously questioned whether an examination of Catholic and non-Catholic immigrants would reveal conditions so disproportionately unfavorable to Catholic immigrants as one might conclude from certain explanations that have been given in connection with the present problem. It must be conceded, however, that the development of American Catholic life from immigrant origins has been complicated by the partial segregation of the Catholic community and the partial alienation of American Catholicism from important aspects of American secular culture. At this point the question might be raised as to what extent intellectuals were actually produced from immigrant Catholic origins but were lost to the Church by apostasy.* Certainly the objective segregation and disarticulation we have examined would suggest that this may have been so. It is doubtful if such cases are numerous, but numbers would not be the most important criterion for judging the problem, since intellectual groups are always a minority in any population.

Two further aspects of this situation have at times been suggested. The first is that a great majority of Catholic immigrants not only had to enter the American social system with lower-class status, but they also came from peasant backgrounds in Europe. Hence the problems inherent in the assimilation of a lower-class Catholic group to a Protestant-derived culture were complicated by the problems of a peasant group adapting itself to urban life. This has certainly been involved in our difficulties in the past century. But this, as well as the other factors we have considered, must be kept in perspective. It must be stressed that immigration, with the exception of newcomers from Puerto Rico and from the ranks of displaced persons, has not been an important aspect of American life for more than a generation. The year 1924 saw important legal

---

* Some importance, for example, must be attached to the fact that, to cite one field alone, so many major American literary figures are lapsed Catholics.

changes which put an end to more than a century of relatively free immigration to this country. In fact, for large numbers of American Catholics, immigration has become sufficiently a thing of the past for them to oppose liberalization of the immigration laws.

Let us further note that in the 124 years from 1820 to 1943, some six million Germans and four million, six hundred thousand Irish came to this country. The Germans were Protestant in a majority of cases, although the Catholic minority was of considerable proportions. The Irish were overwhelmingly Catholic. In the same period four million, seven hundred thousand Italians came who were, at least nominally, Catholic almost to a man. The peak year of German immigration was 1882, that of Irish immigration 1851, and that of Italian immigration 1907. In other words, the peak year for the most recent of the three most important Catholic groups of immigrants was half a century ago.

The Poles comprise another important Catholic ethnic group. Their peak year for immigration was 1921, when four hundred fifteen thousand Polish immigrants arrived. Thus even in the case of the Poles, the peak year was over a generation ago. Moreover, this figure is deceptive. It must be recalled that Poland had been deprived of independent national existence for a long time prior to the First World War. That means that Polish immigrants came to the United States before that time as Russians, Germans and Austrians. The peak year for Austria-Hungary was 1907, for Russia, 1913.

Thus, the peak decade for Catholic immigration as a whole to this country was that of 1900-1910, almost half a century ago. It certainly seems rather late in the day to attribute to immigration and the immediate problems of assimilation the chief influence upon the evident problem.

The decline of intolerance and nativism is too evident to need any documentation, despite the regrettable rise of new Catholic-Protestant tensions recently and the anxieties of those non-Catholics who imagine they see "Catholic aggression" in this country today. There is evidence from recent studies which indicates that in business leadership and economic status Catholics have improved their condition considerably in the recent past.[4] Plainly, therefore, both the factor of intolerance and that of economic hardship must receive reduced emphasis as present causes contributing to our problems.

What these considerations suggest is that the present problems of developing an adequate intellectual life among Catholics in America are not to be identified to any significant degree with those that characterized our history up to now. They are rather the products of that past. That past lives on, not in the forms that it displayed fifty or one hundred years ago, but rather in what we have inherited from that past experience and development. It is in present-day attitudes, in contemporary values, in current definitions of the situation, that the past history of American Catholicism persists in the present.

The partial segregation of Catholicism from basic elements of the general American culture, the over-identification with other elements, the defensiveness, the definition of life in terms of getting ahead in the new world, the odd divisions of labor between clergy and laity, the lack of a continuing tradition that gave a place of honor to intellectual pursuits—these are some aspects of our past history which affect our present. The past affects the present in those forms in which it exists in the present. It exists in the present, objectively, in terms of contemporary social and cultural patterns and, subjectively, in terms of attitudes operative in the here and now although formed in the past.

Thus, we cannot blame too much of our present upon the difficulties which Catholic immigrants found in assimilating themselves to America. Experience of living among American Catholics, as well as the general level of American Catholic life as it meets the eye of the casual observer, suggests that in *non-intellectual* areas American Catholics have not been late in assimilating themselves to the national milieu. The taste for automobiles, the styles of clothing and hair-dressing and use of cosmetics, the felt necessity for radio and television, the interest in movies and sports—in short, all the other indices of superficial conformity—seem to be quite visible in the American Catholic scene. Catholics have not been slow to accept what are often called—especially by our Catholic intellectual brethren in Europe—the more materialistic aspects of American life. Catholics, laity and clergy alike, have been able to come to terms with these aspects of modern America, although it seems possible that on a deeper level some of them deserve more critical examination by the Christian conscience.

A casual observer might further note that a considerable proportion of the diocesan press reveals at times serious hostility towards certain aspects of non-Catholic culture in this country. Yet such hostile treatment—often rather belligerent, let us add—of aspects of American culture that create difficulties for Catholics often conveys at the same time the impression that only Catholics—in fact, only Catholics who share the writers' opinions, plus one or two prominent non-Catholic spokesmen who agree with them—are true Americans. Such journalistic examples are evidence of the over-identification with America in a formal sense while evincing the signs of alienation from other aspects of American culture.

The important point to be stressed here is that the problem we face is a contemporary problem and calls for analysis of those contemporary factors which today inhibit the development of a native Catholic intellectual life proportionate to the numbers and resources of the American Catholics. These factors and their operation at the present time will occupy our attention in the chapters to follow. In that analysis we shall refer to the American past only to the extent that may be necessary to throw light upon the origin and evolution of these contemporary factors.

CHAPTER V

Latent Culture Patterns of American Catholicism

Part 1: How Important Is the "World"? Is It "Dangerous"?

Part 2: Have We Lost the Sense of Quest and the Sense of Mystery?

Part 3: Lay Christianity and American Social Mobility

Part 4: Do We Avoid the Problems of Maturation?

CHAPTER V

Latent Culture Patterns of American Catholicism

In our discussion of manifest Catholic culture patterns (Chapter II, Part 4) we considered, along with the explicit teachings of the Church, explicit Catholic attitudes which might possibly qualify or even distort and subvert the teachings themselves. We found in addition that many times we were dealing with attitudes which might not be entirely explicit but nevertheless produced their effects in the general atmosphere surrounding the more clearly defined attitudes. In the present chapter we shall develop this line of investigation further and consider the latent content of Catholic culture patterns in America in their relation to the intellectual life.

These are more obscure orientations which grow out of the American Catholic situation and which can pervade the general approach we have to the problems of life. Despite their subtle and implicit character, they are of first

95

importance. In fact, precisely because they are less accessible to examination and are often communicated indirectly by cues, by example, and by unconscious implication, they may speak more loudly and more effectively than our words. The subtlety of this area of cultural analysis is such that only careful research could uncover all the problems involved. The best we can do here is to suggest the historical background out of which such latent culture patterns really develop. This we shall attempt to do by asking certain questions and trying to determine how our answers to them have been dictated by historical circumstances rather than by a full examination of problems as they exist today.

Part 1: How Important Is the "World"? Is It "Dangerous"?

One important aspect of the tension between Christianity and the world reveals itself in the problem of maintaining a proper hierarchy of ends. Catholic philosophy sometimes rests content with an architectonic solution to the problem, affirming the value of nature and its subordination to and fulfillment by grace. Such solutions are helpful so far as they go, but what is actually needed by the person who acts in a real-life situation is a working solution—or equilibrium—for the tensions produced by demands and calls directed to him by values and ends whose significance must be weighed by the Christian in the light of his religion. Ultimately, of course, such problems are solved by the development in the individual of prudence, a virtue of the practical reason.

Problems of this kind are many and highly ramified; here we are concerned with recording the fact that the lay American Catholic who must make a concrete Christian way of life for himself often finds himself on a veritable frontier when he attempts to relate his worldly occupation to the inner meaning of the Christian life. The work to be done in society is not in any practical, realistic sense perceived by most Catholics as a structure of potential vocations, and it is not always easy to see it as such. The priest and the religious are called through their professions. The layman is called, it sometimes seems, in spite of his.

Such a definition of the layman's lot and of life in the world is often only implicit in the great body of Catholic writing; at least it is not part of explicit teaching on a high level, although it may be conveyed in certain kinds of sermons, devotional tracts, etc. The absence of a developed theology of work, or of a theology of the lay life in the world, is, however, an eloquent if silent testimonial to the nature of the situation. Throughout its career the Church has been under both obvious and subtle pressures to reject the world and the flesh. Throughout, it has stood fast, and in terms of the enunciation of Christian doctrine it has always refused to yield to these pressures. Yet on the practical level these pressures have had their effects. The concrete conditions of Christian life over the centuries have inhibited the development of lay spirituality; they have also, at some times and in some places, created a breach between clergy and laity and thus have been the cause of apostasy.

In the early Middle Ages the life of the monk became the concrete embodiment and the model of the Christian life.

Alongside this ideal the Church accepted a norm—regarded as a lesser good and a compromise—for the Christian who did not leave the world to live under a monastic rule. This "compromise" governed the Christian lives not only of the laity but in most instances of the secular clergy as well. Later on, with the growth of trade and the rise of the cities, the Middle Ages saw the emergence of a lay culture and with it the establishment of political liberty. The layman was coming of age. This development in the medieval commune produced in many instances something that looked more like a Christian lay society than anything Christian antiquity had known.

Although this culture, which "from the beginning showed that characteristic of being an exclusively lay culture,"[1] gave impetus to education and created the basis for a great civilization, the higher learning remained to a certain extent a clerical prerogative, and no adequate practical theology was developed to convey the message of the Church to this new lay society. Often the clergy were not aware of the tremendous processes of social change that were at work; or rather, they were not aware of their significance.

Henri Pirenne has commented on this blindness. "Written exclusively by clerics or by monks," he says, the history written in the Middle Ages "naturally measured the importance and the value of events according to how they affected the Church. Lay society did not claim their attention save in so far as it related to religious society. They could not neglect the recital of the wars and political conflicts which reacted on the Church, but there was no reason for them to have taken pains to note the beginnings of city life, for which they were lacking in comprehension no less than in sympathy."[2]

The opportunities for developing a lay spirituality at this time were not absent, had an effective group been in existence to undertake it. For the new lay spirit was, as Pirenne has pointed out, "allied with the most intense religious fervor."[3] The proof of this may be seen in the "innumerable religious foundations with which the cities abounded, the pious and charitable confraternities which were so numerous there."[4] Yet this new class found itself in conflict with ecclesiastical authority that was often too closely identified with the older conservative political and economic elements of the society and opposed the new cities in their bid for political liberty and constitutional government. And as Pirenne has noted, "if the bishops thundered against them with sentences of excommunication, and if, by way of counter-attack, they sometimes gave way to pronounced anti-clerical tendencies, they were, for all of that, none the less animated by a profound and ardent faith."[5] Here we see the beginning of the alienation of the new lay classes from the Church which will become the terrible "normal" condition in our contemporary world.

Since higher theological learning was the property of the educated and since these were largely clerics, this ardent faith was not given the benefit of long and fruitful contact with intellectual developments. Small wonder that the piety of laymen "showed itself with a naïveté, a sincerity and a fearlessness which easily led it beyond the bounds of orthodoxy. At all times, they were distinguished above everything else by the exuberance of their mysticism. It was this which, in the eleventh century, led them to side pas-

sionately with the religious reformers who were fighting
simony and the marriage of priests; which, in the twelfth
century, spread the contemplative asceticism of the Be-
guines and Beghards; which, in the thirteenth century, explained the enthusiastic reception which the Franciscans
and Dominicans received. But it was this also which assured
the success of all the novelties, all the exaggerations and
all the deformations of religious thought. After the twelfth
century no heresy cropped out which did not immediately
find some followers. It is enough to recall here the rapidity
and the energy with which the sect of the Albigenses
spread."[6] Lay piety developed outside genuine contact with
clerical learning in general until the coming of the men-
dicant orders of the thirteenth century. The often related
dream of the Pope who saw the Lateran tottering, held up
by St. Francis and his little brothers alone, was a reflection
of that situation.

In thus failing to understand the developing situation
and the need it presented for a mature Christian lay population, Church leaders were, quite unwittingly, preparing to
lose much of the future. The burghers of the Middle Ages,
laymen yet deeply religious, "were thus singularly well
prepared for the role which they were to play in the two
great future movements of ideas: the Renaissance, the
child of the lay mind, and the Reformation, toward which
religious mysticism was leading."[7]

In any society the strategically influential elites will
shape the formation of those values and definitions of the
human situation in terms of which policies and decisions
are made. In medieval society, the ecclesiastic and monastic
groups were the effective elites, and they failed to grasp the

significance of the new developments taking place among the laity. This difficulty which persons in certain statuses and roles have in perceiving the problems of those in other strata of society is a persistent problem in sociology. As it affected the clergy of the Middle Ages it placed the Church in a position which was later to cause severe difficulties.

As Père Congar has said, "The fact that (in principle) the Church absorbed the world and imposed on it regulations proper to herself eventually meant the ignoring of the secularity of what is secular; preoccupation solely with the last end—the normal point of view of the clergy—led to the disregarding of secondary causes, the proper and immediate causes of things. . . . Medieval Christendom was, very generally speaking, a sacral regime, and by its hold of the spiritual over the temporal it brought about a union of the two that was in some ways premature and bought too cheaply. Earthly things were hardly considered except for their use in the Church's sacred work, hardly at all in their own reality and causalities, and so they were not taken really seriously and received neither the attention they deserve nor the development they call for. . . . Only since the end of sacral Christendom, with its monastic and clerical set-up, have we been able to get the full measure of the extent and requirements of the secularity of things and of the fidelity we owe them."[8]

We all know what happened. Laymen revolted against the Church in two directions. In the north of Europe, they often revolted in order to remain Christian in the face of what looked to them like ecclesiastical secularization and even exploitation. In the south they often revolted in order to assert a confident humanism. Between the two they built most of that civilization of modern Europe and America which has changed the whole world, and in which the Church has remained in the status half of an alien and half of a progenitor. The currents of Protestantism and the Enlightenment which were brought to America, and from which American Catholics have felt so strongly alienated in some respects, derived ultimately from these sources.

Moreover, it can hardly be said that Scholastic philosophy in its treatment of social problems prepared the Church to meet the new and important development of capitalism. Most theological writers—with a few exceptions, such as St. Antoninus of Florence—saw in the new world of commerce and trade not the accumulation of the necessary wealth for the development of a high civilization but simply the attendant social evils.[9] The Church's stand against the outrages of greed and exploitation that accompanied these developments is greatly to its credit. Yet the battle was lost. The result of the failure of churchmen to understand what was actually happening and to relate it to the Christian life was that a secularized modern world evolved in which the sphere of religion was ever more narrowly restricted. The new social classes and strata that emerged were in many instances lost to Christianity or alienated from the Catholic Church.

The process of alienation was complicated by other aspects of contemporary life, lay and ecclesiastical, such as the rise of the sense of nationality; corruption in the Church, and the decline of fervor among the clergy. The result was, broadly speaking, the loss of a devout group which became Protestant and of a humanist group which later became Deist, and still later completely secularized.

Protestantism and Liberalism (in its European philosophical sense) thus resulted in part at least from the failure of the Church's leaders to relate the Christian way of life to the dynamic changes that were in the process of transforming medieval and early modern society. In the event, Church leadership was replaced by a world outlook which secularized all values, since it was based on the experience and the values of lay classes which had developed outside of and away from Catholicism.

These remarks, the purpose of which is analytical rather than descriptive, must not be taken to imply that no lay Catholic culture developed in the Middle Ages, for nothing could be farther from the truth. The statement we have quoted from Pirenne bears testimony to such a development alongside the unfortunate incompleteness to which we call attention. Figures such as Dante, Chaucer, the author of *Piers Plowman* and later St. Thomas More and Erasmus (who although a priest certainly was imbued with much of the lay spirit) bear testimony to the richness of that lay Catholic culture. And in fact English universities not only had laymen within their confines in the later Middle Ages, but in the fourteenth century even offered business courses.

Moreover, the partial clerical monopoly of the higher learning, with its semi-monastic approach to the world, was not the only factor involved in the loss of the layman. It was one among several such factors, but it was—and this is important for our present purposes—one that was not completely resolved, with the result that many of the problems it produced persisted. Furthermore, it is to be suspected that certain of the Tridentine reforms, in a not surprising reaction to Luther's thesis of the "priesthood of all be-lievers," increased this tendency to set the cleric apart and to give him a monopoly of certain aspects of the religious life.

We have considered these developments because they are the background from which many contemporary atti-tudes have emerged. To what extent is our attitude toward the world still influenced by those earlier attitudes? To what extent are we still relegating lay groups to relative un-importance in terms of the Christian life? How much better prepared are Church leaders today to face the new problems that are upon us? Many clerics, especially in America, do not seem to have any deeper understanding of social and historical processes than did their predecessors. The social sciences, history, and the humanities—the intellectual products of the very developments we have been discussing —do not seem to have entered to any great extent into their intellectual formation or brought them into meaningful contact with the world of the educated layman.

We have seen that the failure of her leaders to under-stand the development of lay classes was most costly to the Church in the past, especially with respect to the emergence of a lay intelligentsia and the origins of modern science. Certainly science and humanism grew in soil that centuries of Christian culture had prepared. A. N. White-head has shown how the starting-points of modern science took for granted the basic Christian view of the world.[10] But it is just as certain that despite their Christian founda-tion and the support which was originally given to them by the Church, science and humanism were in large part developed by lay classes increasingly alien to the Christian

view as it was held and propagated by churchmen, and
often in face of ecclesiastical opposition. Science proved to
hold important keys to the future. Hence Catholic thought
not only failed fully to meet the development of the modern world—the world of the layman—with an appropriate
presentation of its basic message; it quite unintentionally
and unknowingly guaranteed that Catholic thought should
enter the modern world on the defensive, and suspecting
evil of much that was new, healthy and great with promise
for the future.

This is not made as an easy or a hasty judgment. It is far
easier to criticize with hindsight than to achieve a policy
based upon genuine foresight. But foresight is what our
present analysis is attempting to achieve. To what degree
do we still see the intellectual world in a way analogous to
the costly misapprehensions of our predecessors?

We have been urged by the Popes—especially the present Supreme Pontiff—to overhaul our thinking in this regard. But to what extent have any large numbers of us
done so? In an earlier chapter we found that many teachers
of religion had not even thought to scrutinize their attitudes and teaching in the light of these Papal pronouncements. If on the manifest and explicit level we find such
situations, what is the situation on the deeper, more implicit level?

The over-cautiousness, the negative moral attitudes, the
desire for conformity, the hedges placed about students'
reading which we found on the manifest level of Catholic
culture patterns all point to the fact that some Catholic
thinking is still being done in the historical framework
from which modern society has long since emerged. It is

obvious how detrimental this is to the development of a lay Catholic culture of richness and profundity. Moreover, such an attitude of defensiveness inhibits spontaneity and threatens originality, both necessary for the development of the intellectual life.

A recent example should be mentioned in this connection. It is well established that Catholics were among the first to explore the possibilities of modern biblical scholarship. But since pioneering in thought and in knowledge means saying something new and involves the possibility of grave error, such Catholic efforts were not well received in some ecclesiastical quarters. Moreover, when the Modernists came forward with what was actually one of the most dangerous heresies to be presented for many centuries, Church leaders, although acting quite justifiably in the defense of the revealed deposit of faith, nevertheless did so in a manner that caused Catholic biblical scholarship to lose ground for at least a generation—a set-back from which it has succeeded in recovering only in the last two decades. The atmosphere—the informal, implicit expectations—in the Catholic milieu was such that creative scholarship was made difficult. This sort of defensiveness has militated in similar ways against creativity in other fields in our own times.

Even a cursory knowledge of history and sociology reveals that institutional systems tend to be conservative. The men who occupy positions in such systems come to define the basic purposes of the institution in the narrow status-perspectives of their own particular roles. Moreover, careerism —often of a subtle and not necessarily reprehensible kind —dictates that many who are not really interested or do not actually understand the issues involved will rally to the narrow definitions of the conservatives. Thus the innovator is seen as a kind of traitor.

Examples can be seen in many institutional systems of a quite various nature. General Billy Mitchell, an early advocate of air power, had difficulties with the Army leadership and was court-martialed. Moreover, a rational, philosophical or even a scientific base for the institution does not rule out such developments. In fact there have been several examples in the history of medicine and also of scientific research. The innovations of Pasteur, Ehrlich and Semmelweiss were resisted, and those of Mendel were neglected to the extent that they had to be rediscovered. It is one of the ever present paradoxes of human life that progressing human activity demands, and actually always tends to establish, institutional structures as a stable context for itself. Yet such structures tend to become rigid and to inhibit creativity, and new advances can at times be made only in resistance to them.

This paradox cannot but affect the Church, since it is on one level a human organization. In fact, since the basic function of the Church cannot be other than a conservative one—to guard the deposit of faith—the problem is further complicated for churchmen. To the essential conservatism of the Church as an institution, there is added the socially conditioned conservatism of the office-holder, whose views, as we have already observed, tend to be molded and circumscribed by his status.

From the point of view of the sociologist there are important analogies between the case of Galileo and that of Mitchell. The defensiveness which the conditions of modern times have forced upon the Church only circumscribes further the views of many Catholics toward the problems that arise. Many Catholics are aware of the analogies between what has at times happened in the Church in face of new situations and similar developments in other institutional contexts—governmental, scientific, and the like. But often they see them only as material for apologetics. The point they make is that the Church in history is on the natural level a human institution, and that therefore we must not condemn it for the blunders characteristic of human institutions. Such misadventures leave the supernatural nature of the Church unimpaired.

While such statements are perfectly true, they represent a completely inadequate response to the issue. For if such confusions and their unhealthy consequences for the Church are to be expected from the nature of the Church, then the rational and intelligent thing to do is to study their causes and attempt to restrict them and their injurious effects. To take any less constructive course is to transform apologetics into a mere apology for our stupidities and shortsightedness, a serious distortion indeed.

The analysis of these latent culture patterns and the role they play in our lives becomes one of the important tasks of Catholic education. But all too often the extreme formalism of that education—the failure of the instructor to disclose the full implications of principles and definitions in terms of the student's experience—not only militates against understanding of the principles themselves but sets up a block to the perception of factual situations. Many Catholics, lay and clerical, in practice often confuse the rational motives for faith and the implications of Christian doctrine with an uncritical conformity to the prejudices of their own concrete social settings. How often, for example, editorials and statements by prominent Catholics on such subjects as psychoanalysis, the arts, international co-operation or technology show less acquaintance with Catholic thought than with lower-middle-class prejudices. In this way is the Universal Church made to look and to act in a provincial manner, and this distorted point of view is presented to the world as Catholicity. Such distortions derive not from bad intentions, but from normal sociological processes. However, these processes can be understood, and to some extent safeguards against them can be developed which will obviate their most unfortunate consequences.

These elements in our latent culture patterns and social structures militate against the development of a vigorous intellectual life among us. On the other hand, only such an intellectual life can provide some measure of the larger view by means of which such unfortunate developments can, in part at least, be avoided.

Part 2: Have We Lost the Sense of Quest and the Sense of Mystery?

Related to our general defensiveness and a further aspect of the formalism to which we have already referred is a peculiar kind of Catholic rationalism inherited from the seventeenth century. Ironically enough, this rationalism outside the Church has definite anti-Christian implications; inside the Church it has—at least in our own day—had anti-intellectual effects. Yet these consequences have not been recognized by many Catholics, who perceive concrete, existential problems only in their technical aspects, which require the attention of the expert in the practical sphere. They tend to think of some of the gravest difficulties affecting the life of society as "merely problems in the concrete order," not affecting "the essential order." They seem to think that no matter what happens in the "concrete order" (where, of course, everything happens that does happen), so long as the abstract philosophical heaven of essences is untouched and uncorrupted, there is no great problem for the Catholic. So long as the Church preserves and enunciates the principles governing right social order, the role of the Catholic is fulfilled. Such is the strange idealism which lurks behind this point of view! In its effects it is indistinguishable from anti-intellectualism, and it accounts, in part at least, for the relative paucity of Catholic writing on and participation in such areas as community relations, urban planning, religious pluralism, the ethics of mass communication and civil liberties.

This philosophical approach seems characterized by a positive addiction to formulae. Correctness of formula often threatens to replace understanding, while rote memorization is held to be the essence of learning. The results are often lamentable. Words replace reality. The effect is often to make it appear to ourselves that we have all worthwhile knowledge and that any further quest is unnecessary. Or that we have explained and shown the rational transparency of all existence and that as a result there are no mysteries to challenge the mind to a cognitive quest. Everything profound is thus rendered superficial and everything that eludes the net of a formula is almost considered nonexistent.

Many teachers of religion seem to see their job as providing a life-time supply of answers to "difficulties" to be memorized and "filed" away for future reference, and often the role of the laity is conceived as that of having in readiness the "Catholic answer" to give to non-Catholic friends. There seems to be an implicit notion abroad in some quarters that the Catholic mind will be the product of the catechism, the scholastic manual, and finally of the pamphlet rack. Too often Catholic college students memorize formulae from philosophical textbooks, formulae which condense the subtle thought of generations of creative effort. It does not occur to some Catholics that profound knowledge cannot really be transmitted in this way.

Knowledge and knowing mean seeing something new, seeing it in a new way, seeing another aspect to reality that one did not see before. Thus while the modern world has been engaged upon the great adventure of science, Catholic thought has often tended to regard such developments as a series of "problems" and "difficulties" to be withstood and met with cautious apologetic compromise. Since in the view of some teachers every Catholic college senior must be equipped to handle all important questions in the field of apologetics, the emphasis must be placed on "covering the ground." A student mentality must be developed in which there are no lacunae challenging original investigation.

One may summarize the issue here briefly as follows: Unless it is possible for a Catholic youth to understand his faith, to know what faith really is, and maintain his faith, without having on the one hand to be spoon-fed when genuine difficulties are involved, and, on the other, having his head jammed with ready-made formulae memorized in

religion and philosophy classes, there is really no hope for
the development of an intellectual life among Catholics.
For to be an intellectual means to be engaged in a quest.
As Aristotle long ago noted, knowledge begins with wonder.
Many Catholic students get an impression that there is
really very little wonderful about their faith—that it is so
close to the rationally obvious that the real wonder is that
outsiders do not see it as such. Such Catholics often seem
to be puzzled by the existence of a long, honorable, and
honestly searching philosophical tradition outside their
own semi-sectarian world. They even express impatience
with it, and feel superior to the "confusions" of modern
thinkers over issues which they themselves have failed to
recognize and too frequently fear when they recognize
them even partially.

Such a frame of mind is based upon quite erroneous implicit assumptions, and such assumptions militate against
genuine and profound Catholic contact with the non-Catholic tradition. The great Protestant and secular thinkers of
America are not just men who made mistakes, like the
"adversaries" of the scholastic manual. They have positive
things to say to those American Catholics who have neglected the search itself. The partial segregation of Catholic
life from that of the general community adds difficulties
in that respect, but further defensiveness concealed under
lethargic self-satisfaction is hardly an adequate response
to the situation. We repeat: to be an intellectual means to
be engaged in a quest, and if to be a Christian has come to
mean to have the whole of truth that matters—albeit in
capsule form—in advance (to know, for example, that
"Plato had an erroneous theory of human nature," that

"Comte held God knows what, which is absurd") without ever having been introduced to a genuine philosophical experience, then we are hopelessly lost.

If the Christian faith cannot enable a man to face the unknown without blinding himself to the fact that the mystery is there; to follow, in the unknown, the traces of meaning accessible to his mind; to live with his face to the existential winds that blow across the great void which modern science has opened up before us in many spheres: then it cannot really be Christian faith. To attempt to substitute for such a faith a worldly human consensus of cultural attitudes is a dishonest—and an unworkable— procedure.

It is quite true, as we have said, that a naive youth can- not be thrown into the depths of modern secular thought to sink or swim. But he can be taught to swim.

These matters need much more empirical investigation than a study of this length can provide, but attempts to study them will meet considerable opposition based upon a fear of frankness and a false reticence in face of reality. The implicit attitudes which constitute the latent culture patterns are an important aspect of the social milieu; they can be the most influential so far as what we are actually doing in respect to the problem under discussion is con- cerned.

We must ask: Is it true that many Catholics are not moved by the intellectual challenge of the modern scien- tific and scholarly world because they are told—implicitly —that they already know everything important—or can know it in capsule form—and that there is nothing fur- ther to look for? Are they also allowed to infer that a genuine intellectual quest is incompatible with faith? Are they taught to accept their faith not as a stimulus to a Christian adventure but as a soporific? Does Christianity, which should act as a Socratic gadfly upon them, actually serve as a kind of intellectual Tsetse fly?

Part 3: Lay Christianity and American Social Mobility

The failure of Church leadership to meet the needs of lay classes created by modern developments is seen in a peculiar form in the United States. The history of this country involves a continuation of that process of social mobility and democratization which de Tocqueville characterized as a "providential drift" of several centuries' duration. Social progress in America has been marked not only by an increase in material means and in leisure for the whole population but also by a progressively higher attainment in terms of formal education and other cultural benefits, such as art, music, literature, etc. As is well known, among the factors which medieval Christianity was not prepared to meet and to understand in the emerging urban civilization of the layman was the factor of social mobility. Medieval Christian thought as a whole conceived the social order as a hierarchic structure in equilibrium, more or less static. The instability which had posed a constant threat to Europe for many centuries after the fall of the Roman Empire had had the effect of concentrating the attention of Christians on the need for order. Order and stability became almost ends in themselves, and change and development were not sufficiently understood. The Christian sense of history to be found in the Greek and Latin Fathers and in the epistles of St. Paul was not related by most medieval thought to the concrete processes of social development. We have seen how the status-conditioned outlook of the medieval cleric had the effect of obscuring these aspects of reality. Catholic thought emphasized ontology rather than history, an emphasis which may have led to an excessive concern with essence at the expense of existence. One important consequence was that the Catholic mind often failed to recognize in the intensified social mobility of the rising civilization a factor full of potentialities for the future; failed to foresee it as the great historic process which, beginning in the early Middle Ages with the development of cities and the manumission of serfs, was to continue into revolutionary modern times and to reach a kind of high point in the prosperous urban American society of our own day.

There are some conservatives today who pretend to see in this process only the vulgarization of culture and the levelling of all values. Such levelling tendencies are undeniably involved, but a sober sociological analysis reveals other, more positive, elements. Man's conquest of nature and his creation of the conditions for a prosperous society can scarcely be said to be without spiritual significance. No one proposes that we return to the unheated churches of the Middle Ages, that we give up modern medical advances, that we substitute for the comfortable home of the common man in America the hovel of the thirteenth-century peasant. Can the mortality rate of the Middle Ages before scientific control had been established over epidemics be considered a positive value? Here again we must not take refuge in verbalism. While we must not be unaware of the corrupting and corroding factors in modern developments we must also realize that in this country, capitalism, democracy, science and a faith in the common man have laid the foundation for a social order which goes further toward meeting the standards of Christian humanism than that of any era in the history of the world. Yet the basic processes of social mobility which have issued in these developments were not recognized for what they were even by some of the greatest Christian thinkers of past centuries. They counselled instead contentment in one's station here below; many of the scholastics conceived the desire to rise in status as an evil.

In this country the Church did implicitly encourage social mobility. It was closely associated with, and affected by, the aspirations of Catholic immigrants, and even in their status-conditioned perspective the clergy recognized that the Americanization of the Church depended upon the upward social mobility of its members. But the fact remains that this recognition was more a matter of practice than of precept. Explicitly and in theory the Church in America came no closer to a confrontation of the great "providential drift" than had the Church in Europe. It never faced the theological problem posed for the Christian life of the laity by this factor of social mobility. The clergy, which continued to do most of the thinking for the Catholic community, did not see this problem as one of those demanding its attention. And since social mobility was among the most significant processes at work in American culture, failure at this point meant in large part a failure to come to grips with America and its spiritual significance. The result has been that a concrete Christian way of life built around this basic American process has not appeared. There has not been developed, for example, a "spirituality of the suburbs," if we may use that term. One of the consequences is that there has been produced and maintained in the American Catholic mind a cleavage between the sacred and secular spheres.

This divided Catholic mind has not been able to seize in its wholeness the problem presented by life in American society. It has been intent on a cautious morality confined to certain areas, while aspects of American life which superficially are morally neutral but are in fact full of possibilities for spiritual damage in the long run are left unevaluated. Outside the narrow moral sphere which American Catholicism has taken as its central province, the American Catholic is assimilated to the materialistic society about him in some of its most pernicious aspects. It is for this reason that middle-class Catholic ideals so often appear to be false, shallow and derivative. Catholics tend to be imitators of non-Catholics in everything from educational procedures to tastes in house furnishings, but they do not always show much understanding of what is best and most worthy of imitation in the culture of non-Catholics. Catholics in sermons and editorials often decry the "materialism" of our age, but it is not always clear what they consider that "materialism" to be. Indeed, the hypothesis proposed here is that outside a specifically religious, and often quite closed-off, sphere of consciousness which we may designate as "sacred," American Catholic middle-class life often tends to be more materialistic than is that of many Protestant and secularist groups. That is one reason why learning, which does not receive great material rewards in this country, and the learned professions, which often demand material sacrifices, make a considerably weaker appeal to Catholics in comparison with many other groups, while a very high proportion of Catholics enter the comparatively lucrative professions of law and medicine. It is not the only reason. But it is one that deserves attention from us. There is evidence to suggest that large numbers of American Catholics do not understand the possibility of any kind of genuine vocation outside that strictly segregated "sacred" sphere. Learning, the arts, literature—these fields offer little attraction in terms of Christian vocation to these people. This naturally intensifies the tendency to see the clergy as the thinkers, while the laity devote themselves to worldly tasks which they try to keep as morally innocuous as circumstances permit.

Part 4: Do We Avoid the Problems of Maturation?

Certain aspects of Catholic culture patterns in this country, both on manifest and on latent levels, have been examined in order to reveal the motives and ideals which are operative in the American Catholic community. We have endeavored to uncover what is expected and acceptable, what lies at the bottom of certain Catholic attitudes, what the actual context of Catholic behavior is beneath the words and expressions which play the double role of expressing and concealing the deeper latent level. These basic attitudes, despite their indirect expression in most cases, will have the most important influence upon the socialization process and the formation of character.

Thus, from one angle our study of American Catholic culture patterns is a study of the factors which shape the personality structures of our young people in the course of their development. Here we shall be concerned with the effect of these patterns—especially their latent content— on one aspect of personality development. What is the effect of these factors upon the growth to maturity?

Contemporary American society is based upon education, science and the exploitation of technology, and made up of diverse groups and values. In such a society adult attitudes and behavior require calmness in face of confusion, patience with one's own ignorance, reasonable attitudes toward differences, and flexible action in meeting the unexpected. Balance and levelheadedness in face of new situations, and moral integrity, together with tolerance for honest differences, are most important. To these must be added the ability to sympathize with those whose background and experiences may be quite different from one's own.

The achievement of maturity requires successful mastery of the concrete problems which life presents to the growing person. Maturation is a process marked not only by continuity but also by radical discontinuities, which are often experienced subjectively as crises. Such crises mark transition points, and the way in which they are met is of vital importance to the future psychological, intellectual and moral health of the person. Yet American Catholic culture often seems implicitly to encourage an evasion of these necessary crises so far as is possible. What is suggested here is that the verbalism and the defensiveness so characteristic of much of American Catholic life result in a refusal on the part of many to face frankly and honestly the risk of growth in the psychological and intellectual sense.

Just as the great adventure of modern man, the scientific exploration of the unknown, is too often seen by American Catholics as a vain quest since they already have the whole of essential truth, or as a source of "difficulties" to the faith which must be counteracted by nice formulae, so, it is suggested here, the great adventure of the adolescent, the exploration of the new world of adulthood opening out before him, is often treated as one in which a cautious resistance to change is best, or in which challenges are seen as difficulties to be got around with as little risk to the ideas of childhood as possible.

To be an adult Christian means the growth to maturity of one's Christian outlook as well as of other aspects of the personality. To make the transition from the faith of childhood to that of manhood involves drastic discontinuities: when the stage of childhood has come to an end, there is often an hiatus, marked by intense emotional and intellectual tension, before the stage of manhood can be entered by the re-integrated personality. But it seems as if American Catholic culture patterns and practices often encourage the avoidance of such normal crises of personal growth. One is led to suspect that the improper handling of these crises may be a prime source of leakage to the Church, and such leakage is terribly damaging because often it is people of genuine intellectual caliber who are lost.

Sometimes one is told by priests that youths are lost at

this time because of moral and not because of intellectual difficulties. A diagnosis in terms of such a facile "either/or" often seems completely unrealistic. These crises are of a mental-emotional-moral nature, as in fact are all crises, and they are part of the normal growth process. They must be understood and dealt with as such. To see them merely as the result of moral problems is the survival of that medieval mentality which looked on the heretic as always in bad faith, combined with seventeenth-century rationalistic psychology.

Monsignor Romano Guardini has written an article that contains a great deal of insight concerning "Faith and Doubt in the Stages of Life." He has shown how each stage involves its own peculiar religious and moral problems and how each at the same time presents a challenge and an opportunity for spiritual growth and development. Calling our attention to the important discontinuities involved in growth, Monsignor Guardini writes: "Human development runs along not evenly but in segments. The child's condition of soul does not merge gradually into that of the youth, or the youth's faith into that of the mature person; each stage is characterized by its distinctive form. These forms do not slip easily from one into the other; the new form supersedes the earlier one. To be more explicit, it is rather like this: the first form develops, finds expression in the ways of thinking and feeling and in dealing with things and people. Meanwhile, the new form is in the process of taking shape below the first. Then the new form breaks through more or less suddenly, and affects the person's whole nature. In every case a reconstruction is involved— often even a violent shattering of the old form. On the other hand, it is the same life fulfilling itself. All that one had experienced, learned, and appropriated remains, and bears the stamp of the preceding period. Thus arise tensions, complications, ambiguities and contradictions—crises of development. Since it is not an abstraction who believes, but a real, living person, these changes affect faith itself, and become religious crises."[11]

The hypothesis proposed here is that American Catholicism—except in the individual work of certain thoughtful priests and sisters—does not meet these crises with anything like adequacy. It fails to recognize them as normal, and by its defensiveness and its verbalism it inhibits a fruitful working through of them. It is oriented to smoothing out difficulties instead of meeting and overcoming challenges, and as a result it fails to integrate such crises into a pattern of spiritual and intellectual growth for its youth.

Why is it that converts seem to be more creative in intellectual activities than so-called "born Catholics"? Is it because they have gone through the necessary crises of growth? Is it that such crises have often been evaded by "born Catholics" and therefore a comparable maturity is not reached and comparable creativity is not produced? Some Catholics respond to a discussion of this kind by saying, "Yes, that is all well and good, but won't a lot of people lose their faith?" What strange half-conscious attitudes such fears reveal! The latent culture patterns involved imply that faith cannot stand growth. The risks are real, and no attempt should be made to minimize that fact; but the potential for growth is no less real, and it too should not be minimized.

It is suggested here as a working hypothesis that as a

result of the failure to relate social mobility to the spiritual life in any but an extrinsic way, and the failure to develop institutionalized culture patterns to enable Catholic youth to meet the crises of growth openly and with beneficial consequences, immaturity in the cultural and intellectual sense is one of the striking characteristics of American Catholicism as a whole. Hence the American Catholic community not only fails to produce an intellectual elite, but even tends to suspect intellectuals because American Catholics sense the relation of the intellectual to these two partially repressed American problems. The intellectual symbolizes in some way the facing of crises and the challenges of uncertainty, as well as a critical attitude toward the accepted values of middle-class life, especially those which are most crassly materialistic. Catholics, who pride themselves on their spirituality, are more prone to support anti-intellectualism than are many other of their countrymen. They see the intellectuals as those who seek to reveal the basic existential ambiguities that they themselves wish to evade. They often project this dilemma onto current politics and see such intellectuals—who are in our culture, for all the reasons we have examined above, often liberals —as "disloyal." One sometimes feels that for some Catholics "loyalty" is so supreme a virtue that it would be disloyal and almost sacrilegious to ask, "Loyalty to what?"

For such Catholics this too is an intellectual-emotional-moral problem. To the extent that faith—not the verbal arguments for it but the real intellectual hold on it—is weak, to that extent the intellectual is seen as an enemy. If one's life is projected upon the fragile bridge of a superficial faith, then any criticism becomes a severe threat. Any atmosphere in which Catholic values are not taken for granted—not simply not violated in practice but never challenged—becomes dangerous. But in our society, in view of the last four hundred years of Western history, Catholic values are bound to be challenged in most intellectual circles. If the Catholic is not prepared for this, he is simply not prepared for life.

If the Catholic has an immature faith and many unsolved, partially repressed problems in his own mind, then the intellectual critic becomes the external surrogate of the repressed interior questionings, and the well-known psychological mechanism of displacing aggression and guilt ensues. One sees a good deal of what looks like this—the rigidity and hardly disguised panic are telltale signs—in American Catholic life, but such Catholics, often the victims of their facile and superficial rationalism and verbalism, do not seem to see what is going on. If one has repressed the unsolved problems at one of the crises of transition to which modern psychology has called our attention, one will of course have one's intellectual difficulties compounded with psychological ones, and often with moral ones.

From these problems the Church suffers two important kinds of loss. First, there is the positive secession of potential intellectuals among our youth. Some of them go on to become important in the cultural scene. Every sensitive parish priest can tell you of this kind of problem. Secondly, others, who do not revolt, sink into a kind of stultified intellectual lethargy, avoiding dangerous areas of thought or life; or they may fail ever to have had their intellects vitally engaged in living at all. This last category is not necessarily confined to laymen. Such persons may channel their energies into other areas, but it is to be suspected that their activities in those areas are often unrelated in anything except the most residual way to the life of faith which they continue in terms of the performance of the required practices.

Certain aspects of this problem may be seen again in many Catholic utterances and even in Sunday sermons in some parts of the country. What is most noticeable is the relative absence of the presentation of the great dogmas of the Catholic religion in preaching and writing, combined with a great deal of unwarranted dogmatizing on all sorts of unessential questions, precisely in fact in the areas where the Universal Church leaves the Catholic explicitly unbound and urges him to use his own judgment. Persons in this category dogmatize about everything from the Fifth Amendment to psychoanalysis, although their knowledge is usually not proportionate to their misdirected zeal. Such behavior is found unfortunately among clerics as well as laymen. It deserves to become the object of serious study. If such attitudes are in fact widespread in the Catholic milieu, and if they make up a considerable part of the latent content of Catholic culture patterns in certain areas of this country, then it is small wonder that no intellectual stratum of sizable proportions has emerged.

CHAPTER VI

The Social Structure of American Catholicism

Part 1: Clergy and Laity in America

Part 2: The Prestige Status of Catholic Groups in the Secular Society

The Social Structure of American Catholicism

In considering the social structure of American Catholicism it will be necessary to bear two distinctions in mind: the distinction between laity and clergy; and the social distinction between the Catholic community and the rest of the population. First, we shall look at the structure of the Church and its lay organizations in this country; second, we shall look at the social stratification of the Catholic population. The second inquiry will concern itself with the distribution of Catholics among the social classes in the country and the social prestige accorded Catholic groups and the various ethnic groups from which Catholics come.

Within the Church itself there are two definite strata, the clergy and the laity, whose relations to the functioning of the Church—the administration of the sacraments, the liturgy, worship, and the teaching apostolate—are, and have traditionally been, distinct. Rooted in distinctions already to be found in the Gospels, the Acts of the Apostles and the Epistles of St. Paul, this division into strata had by the second century evolved two recognizable social orders within the Church. Certain specific historical experiences of the Christian body imparted to these concrete social structures a content which tended to increase the difference in function and the social distance between them.

In addition there evolved in time another stratum within the Church which to some extent cut across the existing strata to create a third grouping. The second and third centuries saw the rise of monasticism. Resisted at first, the monastic order, embodying the counsels of perfection of the New Testament in a life of renunciation of the world, eventually came to be recognized as a way of life superior to that of the world. One result was the tendency for a double pattern of life to be set up, with one, higher, level of spirituality required of religious and another, lower, level required of those "in the world."

One residue of this long historical experience is the attitude which still conceives vocation almost solely in terms of religious or clerical life and leaves the life of the laity in an important sense largely unregulated by the principles which should inform a genuine vocation recognized as such. Another is to be seen in the attitude which would give to the priest or the religious a kind of monopoly of the activities that involve learning and the more serious intellectual and spiritual interests. There is strong evidence to suggest that these two long-term tendencies in Catholic culture continue to prevail in the social structure of the Church. Several years ago a Catholic sociologist made a study whose results showed that Catholics do tend to carry over the paternal relationship of the priest to the layman into spheres where it is inappropriate and may discourage the proper initiative of the layman.[1]

Part 1: Clergy and Laity in America

The original distinctions, as they assumed institutional form in the second century, tended to make the clergyman the teacher, initiator and conserver in the intellectual sphere. Monasticism also in time assimilated some share of these functions to itself. In America, where for years the lay Catholic was usually an immigrant, such tendencies could not but gather force. The question therefore arises: to what extent do these distinctions between priest and layman, and the reciprocal expectations derived from them, constitute an element in the problem we are considering?

There is reason to believe that the old expectation that the priest will "know," and that he will take the intellectual initiative when that is necessary, still to a great extent characterizes the relation between priest and laity in the United States. In fact it has been suggested that large numbers of the clergy half-consciously conceive the laity as a kind of spiritual proletariat. They expect little from them in terms of mature Christian knowledge, and in terms of Christian living often not much more than that they will "obey the rules." In some instances which have come to this writer's attention priests have literally been inhibited from expounding dogma in their sermons by fear of upsetting the faith of the laity. They think it safer that educated Catholics should have only elementary knowledge and immature attitudes in areas where educated Protestants may be well informed—for example, in regard to biblical criticism. What such priests think the "faith of the laity" *is* in that sense, and what they think it *ought* to be—the real and the latent definitions—would offer an object of sizeable dimensions to a research project. Such investigatory efforts will, of course, meet considerable opposition from the kind of priest we have described—from precisely those who need it most. Others whose artificially protected background and excessively formalized training have prevented them from coming to grips with the facts will also resist. Some years ago a study of army attitudes during the Second World War was done by social scientists for the War Department. This investigation was resisted by some army officers on the grounds that "a good officer knows what his men are thinking." This is a typical response from those who feel insecure in any organizational structure. We must expect some analogue of it from certain kinds of clerics. But on the other hand most will welcome knowledge which will help them and the laity to carry out the Christian tasks that the Church expects of them.

Some years ago a parish priest was shown a copy of one of Father Fichter's studies in parish sociology by one of his assistants who was a student of the subject. Being a gentleman, the pastor merely said, "I hope you do not intend to make that kind of a study here." Yet one might have thought that it is precisely the kind of information a pastor would want to have.

The experience of the Fordham Sociological Laboratory confirms that many pastors have an intelligent attitude toward supporting and making use of such research. But it must unfortunately be admitted that others raise difficulties. Perhaps the favorite approach of this kind is to put forward so-called "theological" arguments. "After all, one cannot study the effects of grace empirically." Such a retort has little bearing on the issue, and one wonders what those priests think has been going on in history, the humanities and the social sciences for decades. Defensive reactions of this sort tell us much about the latent expectations in some clerical circles; and they also demonstrate how the structure of the clergy, like all occupational and professional structures, can show in places and at times the tendency of the "office-holder" to avoid facing unpleasant facts which may reveal his weakness to himself and his colleagues, even though consideration of them might help him be more efficient in his tasks.

This tendency of many among the clergy to see the laity as needing no advanced religious knowledge—in fact, to feel that it is safer for all concerned if they do not have it—actually does an injustice to the Church. Often the clergyman, busy with his own tasks and conditioned by the selective view of his calling, is slow to see the significance of these issues. I have talked to theologians who, although they thoroughly approve of the new attitudes toward teaching theology to laymen, do not seem at all disturbed that this development should have been so long in coming.

The theological and philosophical preparation of many clergymen has evidently not rendered them aware of what are actually long-term trends in our civilization. Either the fact that it is impossible to produce intelligent Christian laymen without conveying by education an adequate intellectual grasp of Christian thought has never occurred to them, or it has occurred to them but they are opposed to such a course. In most cases the difficulty is the former one, but both offer examples of "clericalism." Clericalism, in this sense, means to be so bound by the status-conditioned view of the office that it becomes impossible to see general problems whole, or with detachment. The result is that the initiative of the Catholic layman may be distrusted by the clergy, while the non-Catholic layman builds a great secular civilization. The problem this presents is serious because it means that members of the clergy so affected have no real grasp of what is going on in the world, no comprehension of what has caused the great set-backs which Christianity has suffered.

Are there perhaps elements in the preparation and formation of the clergy that develop and perpetuate these attitudes? As several observers have already pointed out, the priest is often given a highly formalized education combined with a highly segregated spiritual formation.* The consequence may be that little sympathy for the intellectual quest is produced in the student priest, who is thus inadequately prepared to interest himself in and to grasp the problems facing man in the modern world.

Earlier (Chapter III, Part 2) we discussed the kinds of problems which need investigation in connection with Catholic education. The latent level of such problems will be found to be the more important, for the attitudes found in the American Catholic milieu generally must to a great

---

* For a strong statement of this point, the reader might consult the address of Father Gustave Weigel to the Catholic Commission on Intellectual and Cultural Affairs on April 27, 1957. The complete text appears in *Review of Politics*, July, 1957.

extent have their origin in motivations and ideals instilled, sometimes subtly by the very atmosphere, in the elementary school. Is it true that students in the Catholic school tend to feel that because they are taught all or most subjects by a "religious authority" they must accept passively what is given to them? Passive learning, passive acceptance and memorization appear to play a much larger part than they should in Catholic education in religious matters. Is this carried over into the instruction methods for other subjects? Does our Catholic teaching so combine authoritarianism and the verbal formula as to discourage active inquiry on the part of the student? Is such passivity in religious matters mistaken for faith?—if so, an ironic neo-Lutheranism! Does passivity and the memorization of formulae alienate learning from life for our students?* Does the atmosphere of the school so fill them with oppression that they must seek elsewhere for any of the excitements and pleasures of the mind? Is the Catholic classroom the scene of a joint adventure of teachers and students engaged in confronting God's exciting creation? I am unable to answer these questions, but experience with Catholic faculty members, both clerics and laymen, convinces me that they should be asked and that they deserve investigation. For the Catholic college instructor frequently complains that in all too many cases the attitudes of his students seem to have been conditioned by just such a background as we have proposed for consideration.

A further complication of our problem may be the sys-

---

* For an interesting presentation of this view, the reader is referred to the article on Catholic college education by Daniel and Sydney Callahan in *The Catholic World*, December, 1957.

tem of promotions in clerical and religious circles. In every social system we find what sociologists call the institutionalized reward system. There is, moreover, in any institutionalized promotion system, as an unintended concomitant of the very necessary stability that institutionalization provides, a tendency to reward in some form everything that does not threaten the *status quo.*

A great deal of concrete research in administration has been done by American business organizations precisely on this kind of problem. Certainly the Church will not be any less fearless than such worldly organizations in supporting research to aid its creative self-criticism, as it has already done in the well-known "management audit" of several years ago. Yet too often the very cautious administrative attitudes we wish to study may tend to prevent such study. Some time ago I said to some Catholic sociologists that an important part of any sociological study of institutions was to understand what factors, manifest and latent, affect promotion. When I suggested that this would be a good topic for study in connection with the Church in America, one sociologist who is also a priest agreed but said, "You'll get into trouble if you try to study that." Such attitudes speak volumes if they really are representative of large numbers of administrators.

Related to the problem just discussed is the question of what distortions we have permitted to develop in connection with the conception of Christian obedience. Is it true that in some instances Christian obedience tends to degenerate into the obedience of the military life, or of the unintelligently conducted business firm? I say "unintelligently conducted" because large business shows much more regard for personality factors in the issuing of orders than some of our ecclesiastical bodies seem to do, if some reports are to be believed; and the continuing social-science research supported by business in this regard is an important element of the picture. "Seeing Christ in the religious superior" places a tremendous responsibility on the religious superior unless the main purpose of the relationship is purely penitential for the subject. How often in our religious communities are talents in some important field wasted or left undeveloped because the superior must have a teacher of business subjects, to meet a lower-middle-class demand, or some minor organization must have an administrator? Many similar problems could be raised, and we have alluded to some of them in previous chapters.

One sometimes feels that American Catholicism runs the danger of so overemphasizing the principle of authority as to annihilate the equally vital principle of community which should be its complement. The results of such a deformation can be devastating. Take one example. If a creative theologian should say something that is criticized by authority, this is immediately interpreted by many Catholics—lay and clerical—as meaning that the man, or at least his work, "is condemned." Now since there can be very little creative effort without some error, creativity runs the risk of being "condemned" *per se* in these people's eyes. Thus the equilibrium between Catholic community and authority is destroyed.

When in Catholic society these complementary principles are in balance the mode of operation is something like this. Between creative thought and authority within the community of the Church there should exist, and essentially does exist, a healthy give-and-take. Authority is charged chiefly with the conservative function—to preserve that which has been handed down. To creative thought belongs the function of exploring the inexhaustible riches of that deposit and its significance for each succeeding generation. Hence the caution and genuine prudence in the statements of Rome on such problems.

Such a healthy tension between these two principles can become the basis for a creative application of Christianity to every period of history and to every contemporary problem. Yet how is this tension often understood in practice among rank and file in the Church? As a kind of law enforcement—the policeman has apprehended the culprit; the young seminarian has been caught by his superior in an infringement of institutional rules. It is very difficult for some priests, even, to overcome these immature reactions. The effect is to encourage the doing of nothing, in the creative sense; to make the intellectual quest seem almost sacrilegious. Such attitudes, to the extent that they do in fact exist, will certainly strengthen the tendency to conceive intellectual activity as incompatible with Christianity. They will reward and reinforce inertia. The existence of such patterns is evident, although their full extent can be known only as a result of further empirical studies. It is to be suspected that such attitudes may play a considerable part in the problems discussed in this study.

Similar kinds of attitudes are found implicit in the relations between clergy and laity. Father Gustave Weigel has written: "The Americans are also strict believers in the distribution of labor. It seems, in consequence, natural that the priest, one of the people, should lead the religious activities of the people." He points out the way in which American life tends to leave initiative to the expert; how in sports events, the players are instructed in every detail by coaches and are expected to obey these instructions. "Hence, it is not surprising," he continues, "that it works in American Catholicism as well. The modalities of older, European-born, pastors who successfully ran their parishes like benevolent despots are no longer popular today and they are a sign of the past. But the modern American pastor does something similar but in a genuinely American fashion. He does not order like a king; he orders like a coach."

Unquestionably such current American tendencies influence parish life, but they build upon the patterns of the past to which Father Weigel alludes. Here we have another example of attitudes from the general American community affecting Catholic predispositions. We saw analogous phenomena in the tendencies toward levelling and the activism which can enter into American Catholic anti-intellectual attitudes.

But it is undeniable that such developments are in marked contrast with other aspects of American life. American soldiers were told over and over again in the Second World War, and there is evidence to support the statement, that the American soldier was capable of initiative and of spontaneously intelligent action when cut off in a small party and isolated from the chain of command. The German and Japanese soldier, according to what we were told, bore a much stronger resemblance to the American parochial situation as Father Weigel describes it than to the American enlisted man and junior officer. He states that "it still remains true that the clergy are all too prone to keep the laity out of tasks of planning, and the laity are only too pliant to accept planning and the competent knowledge for it as the reserve of the priests. There is an energetic passivity in American Catholics, but they are weak in initiative."[2]

American writers and speakers have always attributed the characteristic of initiative to the democratic character of American life and to American free enterprise. Studies in the sociology of business bureaucracy suggest that American business men are interested in stimulating initiative and creativity from below and want to understand those elements in organizational structure and bureaucratic attitudes which inhibit it. Catholics can hardly remain indifferent to analogous problems and their solutions.

This lack of initiative which expresses authoritarianism and passivity does not however exclude a disregard for genuine authority when it demands initiative and change. "It is noteworthy that up to the present time, the initiative of the Holy See relative to Catholic Action and the Apostolate of the Laity has not struck too many sparks on the New England scene," said a recent survey of conditions in that area.[3] "It does seem that Catholics in the Northeast are more reluctant to change established patterns than their co-religionists in the Mid-West," wrote another observer. "The recent decree of the new Easter liturgy met with slight response in this area, while it was adopted in many dioceses in the West. Generally, the Mid-West has taken the lead in the liturgical movement, with Chicago, Saint Louis, and Saint John, Minnesota, as recognized centers. The same area has been more active in the successful Cana Conferences and Christian Family Movement to promote a spiritual approach to marriage. A recent survey on the teaching of papal social doctrine in Catholic coleges showed that there was a higher proportion of such teaching in the West than in the Northeast. In the whole field of Catholic Action, while there would be nuances rather than sharp distinctions, one would discover more conservative tendencies in the East, and greater experimentation in the West."[4] It will be recalled that a study of Catholic education discussed in an earlier chapter (Chapter III, Part 2) suggested a similar conclusion concerning regional differences.

This area deserves honest investigation and fearless facing of the problems. For some persons any suggestion of change in this respect arouses the ghost of the old trustee crisis. Yet unless we get more than passivity from the laity, we shall not get spiritual maturity, and without spiritual maturity we shall not produce an intellectual stratum of worth and size.

One recalls the first meeting of President Eisenhower's Cabinet as described in a book published a few years ago. The President, a strong advocate of what he calls the "team," called his Cabinet together to criticize his first inaugural address. When he read it through and was applauded, he responded, "I read it far more for your blue pencils than I did for your applause." He reminded them that "One reason I wanted to read it now is so that you can think it over and be ready to tear it to pieces."[5]

Eisenhower's leadership has been criticized. That of any national leader would be, and in any case not without some justification, for we are all open to criticism. But the President obviously does not feel that his constitutional authority is endangered by his version of the "team." Perhaps this kind of encouragement of initiative in Catholic circles is even more necessary than in many other groups.

At any rate, the intellectual life is not likely to grow in a situation where community is transformed into bureaucracy and where a clerical monopoly of thinking prevails. Moreover, such clerical monopoly tends to damage the quality of clerical leadership itself. If the laity remain the feet and the clergy the head in terms of constructive thinking, then we shall perpetuate a situation that inhibits the development of intellectual responsibility and creativity on the part of all. Such a condition not only inhibits the development of intellectuals but drives potential intellectuals away from and often into antagonism to the Church.

Part 2: The Prestige Status of Catholic Groups in the Secular Society

This topic presents another vast research area, and the problems involved will only be sketched here in briefest outline. Professor Kane[6] has shown that American Catholics, despite observable gains, have not shared in the general social mobility to as great a degree as have American non-Catholics. The evidence suggests that Catholics are heavily concentrated in the lower levels of the social pyramid. This implies that Catholics are not found in large numbers in those social strata whose way of life fosters an interest in intellectual pursuits. For a long period in Western civilization the *rentier* classes have been important in the production of intellectuals. Relatively uninvolved in practical pursuits, with sufficient income and the necessary leisure, and possessing family traditions of culture, such strata offer in many ways the best soil for the growth of intellectually creative individuals.

Although this class is found in greater numbers in Europe than in the United States, it is not unknown in our older metropolitan areas. Catholics are not found in it in any great number, and that is one of the factors inhibiting the development of a Catholic intellectual elite. The upper and upper-middle classes are next in line in the production of intellectually active and creative persons. In these classes also, Catholics are not nearly so numerous as in lower classes.

> Upper and upper middle class families provide about 10 percent of the children in the United States but send 80 percent to college. The lower middle class produces about 30 percent of American children but sends only 25 percent of them to college. Classes below this provide 60 percent of the children but educate only 5 percent of them in college. Catholics appear to belong mainly to the lower middle and lower class. This has two meanings: they belong to those classes which produce the largest number of children and which provide them with college education to the least extent.[7]

Thus the position of Catholics in the general American stratification system preserves the picture that we saw earlier in the nineteenth century despite recent social mobility. This fact contributes to the severity of our problem. We must recognize the circular causality involved here. The class milieu has an effect upon the ecclesiastical outlook, as people of lower-middle-class origin, clergy and laity, bring the attitudes and latent expectations of their background into the Church and affect Church policies. The resulting policies, by minimizing the importance of the intellectual sphere, inhibit social mobility and tend to keep Catholics in these same classes.

These matters must be given much more attention than they have had among us, and detailed research is of the first importance. Only knowledge and understanding of the concrete situation can enable us to break the vicious circle.

It must be further recognized that in this country Catholics generally descend from ethnic groups whose right to belong has been challenged by nativism in the course of their immigration and assimilation. The resulting lower prestige rating of these groups tends to keep them out of intellectual pursuits which tend to be monopolized by higher-prestige strata. Moreover, their defensiveness can become an obstacle, as we have seen, and their desire to rise quickly can divert them to other ways of life.

One nationality group stands out here as particularly important. The Irish were in many ways the strategic group in relating Catholicism to American life, a fact recorded by all observers of their history in this country. They were the first large group of Catholic immigrants, and in America early arrival has always been of strategic importance. They have produced a disproportionate number of church leaders, priests and prelates. Moreover, their rise to prominence in the Church coincided with a loss in the earlier prestige— tentative though it may have been—that the Church enjoyed in some places in America. It was their immigration in large numbers which fanned the flames of Know-Nothing intolerance. Having come from a background in which

Catholicism had been persecuted for centuries and continued to involve legal disabilities, they found themselves here having to defend themselves against native bigotry. Thus the defensive attitude developed in the old country could only be strengthened in the new. The conditions in Ireland had aligned Catholicism in their minds with rising Irish nationalism, despite the fact that the Irish clergy had not always looked favorably upon resistance and reform movements. For the Irishman the sense of Catholicity and of Irishness blended so that his whole conception of his human dignity became involved in his defense of his religion. Perhaps it would not be too strong a statement to suggest that it was his religion that preserved this sense of dignity in the hard years of penal oppression and poverty before his migration and continued to do so in the new conditions across the sea. The Church became for him the institution that enabled him to naturalize himself in this country, and in so doing he naturalized the Church. But he remained partially segregated from important native currents of thought, as we have seen.

The Irish have been the oldest major Catholic group in the United States; they differed from the majority of Catholic immigrants in that they were already English-speaking; they have been dominant in Church leadership; and they have risen in other spheres of life, especially in politics. Yet the Irish have not produced an intellectual group of the proportions which these advantages would have led one to expect. Why is this? Are the Irish authoritarian to the extent of inhibiting inquiry? Are they more dogmatic in non-dogmatic areas than others? Has their past of oppression made them more concerned with loyalty than with the content of ideas?

The penal code governing Catholicism in Ireland destroyed for a long time the possibility of lay cultured classes, and to some extent that of a nationally educated clergy. It seems unavoidable that the Irish should have brought attitudes derived from this experience with them to America. To what extent has their experience here modified these attitudes? To what extent is the defensiveness we have been describing attributable to them? And has their dominance in the Church retarded the Church as a whole with respect to the development of a Catholic intellectual life here? Certainly Irish American Catholics (of whom I am one) can openly face these questions, which are being raised by American Catholics who are not of Irish background.

Another important source of difficulties may be found in the background of European priests who came to America in the nineteenth century, especially those who composed the faculties of seminaries. To what extent did these, especially the French, bring to this country attitudes formed in the fierce anti-clerical atmosphere of their homeland? Moreover, to what extent did Jansenist tendencies add a disparagement of intellectual activities to the fear of secularism, to make them over-defensive in the attitudes they passed on to their students? The French may in fact have played a double role in this regard, for Irish priests were for generations educated on the Continent, and especially in France. It has been held by a number of students of the period that such priests brought Jansenist inclinations back to Ireland. These questions cannot be further pursued here. Certainly similar questions could be asked of other ethnic groups. Moreover, the peasant background of so many of the immigrants, with which we dealt above, complicates the problems in this area.

From these observations, it is possible to conclude that the status position of American Catholic groups tends to increase the difficulties that we inherit from other aspects of our history. Recent social mobility would suggest that some relief may be granted from that quarter in another generation. But the subject deserves to be carefully studied and research for this purpose to be supported by those genuinely interested in the future prospects of the American Catholic community.

CHAPTER VII

Some Conclusions

CHAPTER VII

Some Conclusions

This analysis has examined from a sociological perspective some of the factors which inhibit the development of an intellectual life among American Catholics proportionate in vigor and extent to the size of the Catholic population.

At the risk of some oversimplification we shall now try to summarize the important factors revealed by our examination. First of all, we have seen that the Catholic world view—the Catholic definition of the life situation of man —while recognizing the important role of the intellect, nevertheless subordinates the intellectual virtues to a more holistic orientation of man towards God. While such a view is not in any sense anti-intellectual, it is under certain circumstances subject to misinterpretation in a more or less anti-intellectual direction.

Secondly, after examining the tension inherent in the relation between the processes of rational criticism and the living of life, we found that intellectual activity, to which our Western civilization accords such value, can and often in fact does come into conflict with man's need for metaphysical security. The intellect in its penetrating, and sometimes relentless, work of "composing and dividing," often cleaves through custom and convention to reveal the unstructured character which man's existential situation assumes when it is viewed in the light of unaided reason. When faith has been allowed to identify itself too exclusively with observance, it becomes dependent upon such finite and ultimately futile human supports, and then intellectual activity can appear to be the enemy of religious certitude. In such circumstances Christians are found aligned against intellectual creativity, scientific innovation and rational and historical criticism. Thus can Christianity be subtly distorted. And by withdrawal from the intellectual sphere, Catholicism, stripped of the intellectual resources which the tradition of the Universal Church would provide, can be reduced from what it essentially is, a fearless and full view of the human situation in terms of a faith which overcomes the world, into a complex of the mechanisms of defense against the metaphysical anguish which a rationalistic view of man's situation would involve.

These larger dimensions of our problem are complicated by sociological factors. A partially segregated clerical class arose within the Church under certain historical conditions, together with relatively isolated religious communities. These groups strengthened the apostolic work of the Church and offered stirring and quite necessary examples of the heroic Christian life embodying the evangelical counsels, but they often had the effect also of producing a cleavage between the full participation of man in the Christian life and his full participation in the life of the world.

This cleavage developed and was accepted by all groups of Christians, though not without protest; and its effect was to give a definite anti-secular cast to Christian orientations. The original Christian indifference to the world had often been subtly transformed in the direction of rejection of the world. While Manicheism was avoided in terms of doctrine, the value of the secular precisely in its secular aspects tended to be lost sight of. Secular intellectual and aesthetic interests did not appear to priests and monks to be of any great importance except where they directly served the ecclesiastical or monastic functions. Such a generalization admits of so many exceptions as to make it all the more important that we should not fail to see the over-all direction of these developments.

As a result of the status-conditioned perspectives of many clerics and religious, a split between the intellectual quest of the Western layman and the religious and ecclesiastical goals of the priest and religious was perpetuated. The counter tendencies in what is in fact a complex set of developments prevented a complete break. Certainly in the seventeenth century many of the great scientists of that "age of genius" were devout Christians. Many, in fact, were members of the Jesuit Order. Yet the general direction of development was not altered, and in the eighteenth and nineteenth centuries the breach between religion and the world of learning widened into a great chasm.

In the American Catholic community, these tendencies to separate religion from the intellectual life were compounded with others deriving from the social and ethnic backgrounds of the Catholic population and from the whole experience of immigration and assimilation within the context of a rapidly advancing industrialization and urbanization. Furthermore, this all took place in the context of the partial segregation which has characterized the Catholic experience in America in relation to the general non-Catholic culture. That situation—one that was the result of unavoidable circumstances—made difficult the development of a creative encounter between Catholic and non-Catholic thought in this country. The effect was to widen the breach between the life of the intellect and religious concerns which historical developments had brought about. Moreover, to the problems that low social status and partial segregation created for the American Catholic must be added those derived from the general defensiveness of Christianity in face of an advancing secularization which marked the eighteenth and nineteenth centuries.

In modern times the problems surrounding the Protestant Reformation and the development of lay culture resulted in a further segregation of seminary education from large and important areas of modern knowledge. Since the clergy was and remains of strategic importance in the Church, that segregation may have increased the isolation of Catholic culture from the developments that have taken place in the general cultural milieu. As a result too many priests remain unaware of the real problems facing Christianity and the Church in the modern world, and actually lag behind the Popes and the American hierarchy. The world outlook of modern secularized man is beyond their comprehension, and in fact they are inclined to consider extremely subtle thinkers outside the Church philosoph- ically uneducated because they do not accept scholastic positions or express themselves in scholastic terminology. The effects of these limitations can be tragic in some in- stances; for example, when a Catholic chaplain to a sec- ular university receives the full impact of the secular- ization and de-Christianization of the past four centuries, and discovers how little weight the arguments from the scholastic manuals calculated to repulse our adversaries actually have for the mind developed by the secular tra- dition.

We may summarize the basic characteristics of the American Catholic milieu which inhibit the development of mature intellectual activity as follows:

1. Formalism

This factor can be divided into two categories.

First there is intellectual formalism, whereby "demon- stration" replaces search, abstractions replace experience, formulae replace content, and rationalistic elaboration re- places genuine ontological insight. Philosophy so taught restricts by its very rigidity the activity of the exploring mind by conducting it only into familiar and shallow chan- nels. Moreover, such formalized mental operations often fatigue the mind and lead to boredom. In this condition intellectual stimuli evoke no real response. Personal ful- fillment through creative thought is inhibited. In terms of religious growth such formalizations remain what they are, external rationalistic defenses. They bear almost no relation to the subjective religious life, to the practice of prayer or to the content of religious devotions. Such formalism and rationalism alienate reason from the inner core of man's spirit.

A second category of formalism can be seen in the Catholic tendency to see the world as "finished," and all things in it as obvious in their essence and meaning. Those things which are of spiritual significance have been clearly labelled for what they are. Outside this sphere, the things which are not immoral are morally neutral. As a result, the life of man in the world, the human enterprise as a metaphysical reality, has no interior relation to the spiritual development of the human person, in so far as it does not involve breaking the rules of morality conceived as quasi-legal formulae. Human fulfillment and Christian fulfillment are not seen as interpenetrating processes. They are separated and even segregated from each other. Thus the secular is not seen as valuable to the spiritual quest of man.

There are two expressions of this tendency to place the elements of life in isolated categories, one religious and the other non-religious. First of all there is the tendency that Father Weigel has criticized in his recent address to the Catholic Commission on Intellectual and Cultural Affairs. Some people see the task of the Catholic intellectual in terms of producing good public relations for the Church and hence miss the importance of intellectual values *per se*.[1] This is what might be called the "devout expression" of this formal segregation. It is found among secular priests, religious and lay people alike.

The second expression of this formal segregation of

what are seen as two compartments of life is the view that since only religious duties and devotions and the demands of morality have spiritual significance, the rest of man's life in the world may and even should be devoted to the ends proposed by worldly values. Since secular activities, in this view, are not related to the basic reasons why we have been placed on earth, and religion has already provided for the mind all knowledge essential to salvation, it seems plain that only an eccentric would embrace learning for learning's sake, when he could devote himself to a calling offering greater material rewards and even greater social prestige. Life outside the specifically religious calling is not a vocation for such people, any more than it is for those in the "devout" category. But their conclusion as to the proper conduct of life might be summed up as: all this and heaven too. This is what we might call the "lay back-bencher's view."

Whereas the "devout" view sees secular values as of no spiritual importance in themselves but as useful for the purposes of ecclesiastical propaganda, the "back bencher's view" sees such secular values as spiritually irrelevant. Both agree that human fulfillment in the secular world is only accidentally related to man's religious destiny. For such people grace in fact is not seen as completing nature; the two are strictly segregated under quite recognizable formal labels. The call of higher secular values in general and of the intellectual life in particular falls here like seed upon stony ground. The social and cultural antecedents of most American Catholics are of a kind to lead many to choose the more materially rewarding course in this kind of situation.

2. Authoritarianism

This factor is expressed in various ways. It derives from a misunderstanding of the role of ecclesiastical authority, and it seeks to impose solutions to problems by the pronouncement of formal statements. But often the problems are such as will not yield to these solutions, perhaps because the complexity of the whole situation is greater than the framers of the solution have allowed for. At times such problems involve questions which each generation, and indeed each person, must state anew in terms of the specific conditions in each case; and the solution must be designed to fit the specific circumstances.

The same factor is seen also in the tendency to rely on the sanction of custom and convention to support majority opinions or the views of institutionalized authority. It combines with formalism to produce a world view in terms of which the statement of a problem bears the solution in it, thus closing the door to lively debate; each thing can be put in its proper category; there is no question which cannot be answered (not to mention the question which cannot be framed): the result is the illusion of a neat universe in which nothing eludes the conceptions of a searching mind. Such a tendency too often subtly penetrates into teaching, preaching and other activities, where it creates quite unintellectual habits of thought. Together with formalism it denudes the conception of the Church of its communal character. It tends to substitute for the Mystical Body of Christ a purely juridical administrative structure. The creative tension between the Catholic scholar and the Catholic community is too often reduced to the relationship between a mischiefmaker and a policeman. Such distortions of the legitimate authority structure of the Church whereby persons in authority take upon themselves all the intellectual functions of the community—which, in the nature of the case, they are incapable of exercising—cannot but cripple genuine creativity.

3. Clericalism

This factor implies that those who make ecclesiastical decisions often tend to see the problems, tasks, risks, and achievements of the Christian life solely from the professional perspective of the priest as an ecclesiastical official. It results in denying to God's creation its proper ontological value. This is what Père Congar has called the inability to see the values involved in the secular as secular. This tendency is increased by that false extension of the monastic outlook of which we have spoken, which sees the secular only as the object of ascetic exercises. The secular seems, in such a view, to have been created in order to be avoided. Such tendencies are analogous to what is found in all human organizations where officials and specialists see the over-all purposes of the organizations in terms of their own role. Clericalism, which is the peculiar form that this tendency takes in a Catholic setting, combines with formalism and authoritarianism to impose its own view upon the laity, who, trained under clerical influence, are passive, although often demurring, in face of such attitudes.

Besides failing to grasp the spiritual importance of the

lay intellectual vocation, it tends to give the priest-role a monopoly with respect to whatever intellectual activities are pursued. Moreover, by creating intellectual dependency on the part of the laity it further inhibits intellectual activity.

4. Moralism

This factor involves the tendency to see the world as devoid of ontological value and spiritual significance but instead to regard it almost exclusively as a place of moral danger to the Christian soul. Creation tends to be viewed as a possible occasion of sin. Instead of presenting a metaphysical challenge and a vocation for the lay Christian in terms of creatures and their significance, life is seen as a series of moral problems. Its dangers are to be shunned. Often such moralism tends toward a kind of ethical formalism or legalism. In such a view life has no real spiritual value, hence the knowledge which, according to Aristotle, all men naturally desire as a central part of that life has none either. From this neo-Jansenism grafted onto a lower-middle-class mentality little can be hoped for in terms of intellectual activity.

5. Defensiveness

This factor derives from a long history of minority status, disability, prejudice and even persecution, and it tends to produce rigidity. All the foregoing tendencies are reinforced by the strongly felt need to repulse attack, whether real or imagined. Moreover, defensiveness tends to keep us from examining our condition in a frank and calm manner. There is considerable reason to believe that such a tendency is giving way in our day to a more secure and more mature reaction to the situation. When we consider the present size of the Catholic community and the progress that we have shown in many spheres of life in America in the recent past, such defensiveness is fast becoming an unworthy sectarianism.

These five factors have been found, often in terms of complex social configurations, to be present on both the manifest and the latent levels of Catholic life in America. However, our analysis has pointed to the great, over-riding importance of the latent level. On this level are to be found the unvoiced and often unrecognized attitudes and orientations which really dictate our actions. On this latent level operate many of the factors which inhibit the development of the intellectual life in the American Catholic community, often working against the manifest and explicitly taught Catholic ideas, values, and attitudes. It is particularly necessary for Catholics to become sensitive to this level of social existence.

Thus the very factors that create our difficulties can prevent our understanding of them. Our formalism and verbalism often lead us into deception—self-deception—while our defensiveness, in making us timid about facing our shortcomings, increases our willingness to be taken in by superficial appearances, when they are more flattering to us than might be the case with the deeper realities.

Here again it is necessary to emphasize the importance

of research. In the course of the present analysis we often had to content ourselves with indications, with tentative interpretations and with hypotheses. Actually what is necessary is general concern over, and large-scale research on, these problems. This should be done from the viewpoints of history, sociology and psychology. Certainly Catholic philosophy and theology need to pay attention to the findings of such research for the readjustment of many of their own at present unsatisfactory positions.

Catholic institutions of learning are the obvious centers for such research, but its importance must be generally realized and the support of the Catholic community as a whole must stand behind it. Certainly some of it would be a worthwhile addition to the seminary curriculum itself. Today all executives—in business and government— have given considerable time, money and personal effort to understanding the problems of organizational functioning and how they affect human personality. Certainly our future pastors and ecclesiastical administrators and educators need similar data, and where except in the development of the social sciences will they find it?

If this examination of the sources of our intellectual shortcomings makes unpleasant reading in one sense, it is, nevertheless, part of a very reassuring development in a far more important sense. This little work is but a single contribution to a dialogue that has been going on within the American Catholic community for some time now. It is a dialogue that has engaged important Catholic figures in public discussion and a much larger number of Catholics, prominent and obscure, clerical and lay, in a good deal of private soul-searching. This continuing discussion is only one sign of the genuine vitality that American Catholic life has been displaying in recent years. It is a real and a deep vitality, and not even the full force of all the old obstacles to vitality will stay it for long. The new movement will, of course, meet with opposition, not only from the factors we have found revealed in this analysis but from the inertia which weighs upon all human endeavor.

This vital concern with our intellectual problems is in fact a part of a general awakening that appears about to burst upon the American Catholic scene. As Father Leo Ward has put it, "There never was a time in the last four hundred years when the Church was advancing on so many fronts as she is today."[2] Since the Second World War there has been an unprecedented growth of the contemplative religious life among Americans, so often presumed to be an activistic people. This growth is shown both in the number of vocations and the increase of monastic establishments. Secular Institutes, Lay Retreat Houses, the Catholic Family Movement, developments in the field of inter-racial relations, the growth of the Liturgical Movement—these are but the most prominent areas of Catholic progress. It is that general atmosphere which provides the setting for the present discussion and for this particular contribution to it.

A second area of Catholic concern, and one that is most closely related to the problem we have been discussing, is our necessity of coming intellectually to grips with Catholic history. As we have seen in this work, the understanding of present problems often requires looking at the course of development which brought them into existence.

Furthermore, it is often important to see oneself and one's problems within the total context of the historical development of which they are a part. As Father Ong has noted, Catholic intellectual life has been slow to assimilate the lessons taught by history. This is another side of the formalism which we found above. "The need for a Catholic appreciation of America in its historical setting," he writes, "arises from the fact that one's intellectual maturity today is tied up with one's insight into and acceptance of one's own history in relation to the whole of history."[3] Only by coming to understand the situations that have formed our present world and our attitudes toward it—especially our latent attitudes—can we achieve anything like genuine freedom from and mastery over the conditioning which such past experiences have produced in us.

Alike in the spheres of culture and social structure, of personal psychology and of history, our greatest need is to break through formalism. What we need most of all is really to become the epistemological realists that we so often formally proclaim ourselves to be. Perhaps history, sociology and psychology represent three general areas—certainly not confined to the academic disciplines which use these names for titles—in which Catholic sophistication needs most to be developed.

All the facts which we have considered take on special and urgent interest when they are viewed in the context of the present position of Catholicism in America and of America in the world. The present hour may indeed be a decisive one for the future of the Catholic Church in America. A new middle class of wide proportions is developing, and with each year the number of students in our colleges and universities increases at a rate that would have seemed fantastic a generation ago. The revolution in public education which began with the invention of printing continues apace in the new media of radio and television. Despite much regrettable banality in the mass media, a genuine popularization of knowledge is taking place.

In addition, the stratum of the genuinely educated is certainly expanding. The vast printings of paper-bound classics, the growing popularity of art reproductions, and the increased sale of musical recordings in recent years bear testimony to that expansion. Men are looking for deeper meanings. Millions of our fellow Americans are searching, often only half-consciously, for more satisfactory values. Although there is admittedly much that is shallow and even false in the renewed interest in religion in this country, there can be little doubt that there is at the root of such developments a serious search for a deeper spiritual life. Moreover, such developments must be seen in relation to a return to an interest in religion on the part of leading intellectual figures both here and in Europe. Today old answers are being challenged by catastrophic events; old solutions are proving unworkable, old compromises are being swept away.

How do Christians meet this situation? Are they a part of this renewed spiritual quest of their fellows? Or are they self-satisfied with a working religious orientation that they think needs no deepening by the present crisis? Do Catholics share in the spiritual reawakening that is coming over so many in Europe and America? And are they ready to share some of the riches of their ancient faith with those outside the Church? Are they exploring those riches in the light of new problems and unprecedented developments? If Catholics remain alienated from the intellectual life of America, if they remain entrenched within their own formulae and aloof from the common life, if they permit themselves to become identified with anti-intellectual outbursts, then Catholicism will fail to meet with the full power of which it is capable the challenge of our times.

Intelligent Catholic participation in the processes taking place in our day—processes that may shape the future of mankind for centuries to come—demands a considerable reorientation of Catholic life. The first requisite for that reorientation is the development of a large and creative intellectual stratum. The defensive mechanisms of yesterday, inappropriate as they already are within the context of our daily lives, take on an inappropriateness of almost cosmic dimensions when viewed in that larger frame of reference. For although it may have been only yesterday in the lives of our older members since such attitudes had a reasonable semblance of congruity with reality, the new day presents quite other demands, and it is most important that Christians should not be found wanting. For our God is also the God of history, and as intelligent creatures of God, men must give an account of themselves in history. Our duty to God, to the Church, to the Republic and to ourselves demands that the present critical reconsideration of ourselves should be carried forward. Let us not be found empty-handed when the bridegroom comes in new historical forms and unprecedented situations.

In 1919, the Catholic Bishops of the United States issued a statement on the social problems facing the nation. That statement makes instructive reading today. When it was issued many well-meaning people considered the proposals it contained far beyond the realm of realization. Today most of its recommendations are in fact well-established and generally accepted aspects of our legal and social system. There is every reason to believe that our present problems with respect to the intellectual life will also be met by forward-looking Catholic policy. The present general concern with these problems in Catholic circles gives us good ground to expect just that in the period ahead.

Notes

Chapter I: STATE OF THE QUESTION

1. D. W. Brogan, *U.S.A.: An Outline of the Country, Its People and Institutions* (London and New York, Oxford, 1941), p. 65.
2. Quoted from John Tracy Ellis, "The American Catholic and the Intellectual Life," *Thought*, vol. xxx, no. 118 (Autumn, 1955); republished in *The Catholic Church, U.S.A.*, ed. Louis J. Putz, C.S.C. (Chicago, Fides, 1956), p. 324.
3. George N. Shuster, *The Catholic Spirit in America* (New York, Dial, 1927), p. 115.
4. John Tracy Ellis, in Putz, *op. cit.*, p. 346.
5. Edward J. Murray, S.T.D., "The Catholic Church in New England," in Putz, *op. cit.*, p. 186.
6. Joseph N. Moody, "The Catholic Church in the Middle Atlantic Region," *ibid.*, p. 198.
7. John J. Kane, *Catholic-Protestant Conflicts in America* (Chicago, Regnery, 1955), pp. 70 ff.
8. Ernest Havemann and Patricia Salter West, *They Went to College* (New York, 1952), pp. 187-188. Cf. Kane, *op. cit.*, pp. 70 ff.
9. Quoted from the *New York Herald Tribune*, February 20, 1958, from the Education column by Terry Ferrer.
10. Kane, *op. cit.*, pp. 57 ff. See also Ellis, *op. cit.*
11. P. 251.
12. John Tracy Ellis, "American Catholics and the Intellectual Life —Some Reactions," *Bulletin*, National Catholic Educational Association, vol. liii, no. 1. (August, 1956), Proceedings and Addresses, 53rd Annual Meeting, p. 110.
13. *Loc. cit.*
14. William L. Newton, S.S.D., "The Sacred Scriptures," in *The American Apostolate*, ed. Leo R. Ward, C.S.C. (Westminster, Newman, 1952), p. 227.
15. Arthur A. North, S.J., "Why Is the American Catholic Graduate School Failing To Develop Catholic Intellectualism?"

Bulletin, National Catholic Educational Association, vol. liii, no. 1 (August, 1956), Proceedings and Addresses, 53rd Annual Meeting, p. 179.

16. Sister Annette Walters, C.S.J., "Why Is the American Catholic College Failing To Develop Catholic Intellectualism?" in *ibid.,* p. 174.
17. John J. Meng, "American Thought: Contributions of Catholic Thought and Thinkers," in *ibid.,* p. 115.
18. Quoted from John A. Lukacs, "Intellectuals, Catholics, and the Intellectual Life," *Modern Age,* vol. 2, no. 1 (Winter, 1957-1958), p. 47.
19. Quoted from Ellis, in *op. cit.,* p. 111.
20. Robert H. Knapp and H. B. Goodrich, *Origins of American Scientists* (Chicago, The University of Chicago Press, 1952), p. 24.
21. Robert H. Knapp and Joseph J. Greenbaum, *The Younger American Scholar, His Collegiate Origins* (Chicago, The University of Chicago Press, 1953), p. 99.

Chapter II: THE GENERAL PROBLEM OF THE INTELLECTUAL

1. Merle Curti, *American Paradox, The Conflict of Thought and Action* (New Brunswick, N. J., Rutgers University Press, 1956), p. 73.
2. Walter J. Ong, S.J., *Frontiers in American Catholicism* (New York, Macmillan, 1957), p. 82.
3. Humphrey J. T. Johnson, "Some Reflections Suggested by Canon 1399," republished from the *Downside Review* (Summer, 1956) in *Cross Currents,* vol. vi, no. 3 (Summer, 1956), p. 210. See also, by the same author, "The Roman Index of Forbidden Books," republished from the *Downside Review* in *Cross Currents,* vol. v, no. 3 (Summer, 1955).
4. Humphrey J. T. Johnson, Correspondence in *Cross Currents,* vol. vi, no. 1 (Winter, 1956), p. 92.

Chapter III: REASON AND FAITH

1. R. H. Knapp and H. B. Goodrich, *Origins of American Scientists,* p. 24. See discussion in Kane, *Catholic-Protestant Conflicts in America,* pp. 57 ff., and Ellis, in Putz, *op. cit.,* p. 347.
2. St. Clement of Alexandria, *Stromateis,* I. v. 28, quoted from

Documents of the Christian Church, ed. Henry Bettenson (London, 1947; New York, Oxford, 1949), p. 10.

3. St. Justin, *Apology*, I. xlvi. 4, quoted from Bettenson, *op. cit.*, p. 8.

4. Tertullian, *De praescriptione haereticorum*, vii, quoted from Bettenson, *op. cit.*, p. 10.

5. Ernst Troeltsch, *The Social Teachings of the Christian Churches*, tr. Olive Wyon (London, 1931), vol. i, pp. 142 ff.

6. Quoted from H. O. Taylor, *The Medieval Mind*, 4th American ed. (New York, Macmillan, 1925), vol. 1, pp. 416-417.

7. *Ibid.*, vol. ii, p. 380.

8. *Ibid.*, p. 421.

9. Philip Hughes, *A History of the Church: The Church in the World the Church Made, Augustine to Aquinas* (New York, Sheed & Ward, 1952), vol. ii, p. 430.

10. *Ibid.*, p. 431.

11. Etienne Gilson, *La Philosophie au Moyen Age*, p. 580, quoted from Hughes, *op. cit.*, p. 433.

12. Hughes, *op. cit.*, p. 434.

13. Lecomte du Noüy, *The Road to Reason*, ed. and tr. by Mary Lecomte du Noüy (New York, Longmans, 1948), pp. 207-208.

14. Herbert Butterfield, *The Origins of Modern Science* (New York, Macmillan, 1951), p. 128.

15. See Giorgio de Santillana, *The Crime of Galileo* (Chicago, The University of Chicago Press, 1954). Also Charles Journet, *The Church of the Word Incarnate*, tr. by A. H. C. Downes (New York, Sheed & Ward, 1955), vol. i, "Excursus VI, The Condemnation of Galileo," pp. 354-358.

16. Alfred North Whitehead, *Science and the Modern World* (New York, Macmillan, 1925).

17. Sister Mary Gratia Maher, R.S.M., *The Organization of Religious Instruction in Catholic Colleges for Women* (Washington, D.C., Catholic University Press, 1951), p. 136.

18. *Ibid.*, p. 138.

19. *Ibid.*, p. 140.

20. *Ibid.*, p. 138.

21. Roland G. Simonitsch, C.S.C., *Religious Instruction in Catholic Colleges for Men* (Washington, D.C., Catholic University Press, 1952), p. 14.

22. *Ibid.*, p. 92.

23. *Ibid.*, p. 141.
24. *Ibid.*, p. 142.

Chapter IV: THE AMERICAN CATHOLIC HERITAGE

1. Carlyle, "Heroes and Hero Worship," lect. iv, quoted from J. L. Spalding, D.D., *The Religious Mission of the Irish People and Catholic Colonization* (New York, 1880), p. 25.
2. Paul Tillich, *The Religious Situation*, tr. by H. Richard Niebuhr (New York, Meridian, Living Age Books, 1956), p. 182.
3. For an interesting discussion see Merle Curti, *American Paradox, The Conflict of Thought and Action.*
4. Liston Pope, "Religion and the Class Structure," *Annals of the American Academy of Political and Social Science,* cclvi (March, 1958), pp. 85-86. Also Herbert W. Schneider, *Religion in 20th Century America* (Cambridge, Harvard University Press, 1952), pp. 227-238. Msgr. Ellis suggests that seminar reports by two of his students on Catholics in business and politics support these studies. Yet it must be recalled that John J. Kane in "The Social Structure of American Catholics" finds that while Catholics do share in the general social mobility, there is "a lack of proportionate upward vertical mobility among American Catholics." He suggests that not discrimination but "some kind of lower-middle or lower-class orientation among them to education and occupation" tends to keep them in the lower socio-economic groups. See *The American Catholic Sociological Review,* vol. xvi, no. 1 (March, 1955), pp. 23-30. Also Chapters V and VI of *Catholic-Protestant Conflicts in America,* cited above in note 7, Chapter I.

Chapter V: LATENT CULTURE PATTERNS OF AMERICAN CATHOLICISM

1. Henri Pirenne, *Medieval Cities,* tr. by Frank D. Halsey (New York, Doubleday, 1956), p. 165.
2. *Ibid.*, p. 100.
3. *Ibid.*, p. 166. Cf. also J. Huizinga, *The Waning of the Middle Ages,* tr. by F. Hopman (New York, 1954), p. 40.
4. Pirenne, *op. cit.*, p. 166.
5. *Loc. cit.*
6. *Ibid.*, pp. 166, 167.
7. *Ibid.*, p. 167.

8. Yves M. J. Congar, O.P., *Lay People in the Church*, tr. by Donald Attwater (Westminster, Newman, 1957), pp. 98-100.

9. See R. H. Tawney, *Religion and the Rise of Capitalism* (New York, Harcourt, 1926) and Amintore Fanfani, *Catholicism, Protestantism and Capitalism* (New York, Sheed & Ward, 1955).

10. Whitehead, *op. cit.*, Ch. I, "The Origins of Modern Science."

11. Romano Guardini, "Faith and Doubt in the Stages of Life," in *The Faith and Modern Man*, tr. by Charlotte E. Forsyth (New York, Pantheon, 1952), pp. 100-101.

Chapter VI: THE SOCIAL STRUCTURE OF AMERICAN CATHOLICISM

1. John D. Donovan, *The Catholic Priest: A Study in the Sociology of the Professions*; unpublished Ph.D. dissertation, Harvard University, 1951.

2. Gustave Weigel, S.J., "An Introduction to American Catholicism," in Putz, *op. cit.*, pp. 18-19.

3. Edward G. Murray, S.T.D., "The Catholic Church in New England," in Putz, *op. cit.*, p. 185.

4. Joseph N. Moody, "The Catholic Church in the Middle Atlantic Region," in Putz, *op. cit.*, pp. 192-193.

5. Robert J. Donovan, *Eisenhower: The Inside Story* (New York, Harper, 1956), p. 2.

6. Kane, *Catholic-Protestant Conflicts in America*, pp. 70 ff.

7. *Ibid.*, p. 77.

Chapter VII: SOME CONCLUSIONS

1. Gustave Weigel, S.J., "American Catholic Intellectualism—A Theologian's Reflections"; reprinted from the *Review of Politics* in *The Commonweal*, vol. lxvi, no. 24 (September 13, 1957).

2. Leo R. Ward, C.S.C., "The Church in America," in *The American Apostolate*, p. 2.

3. Walter J. Ong, S.J., "The Intellectual Frontier," in Putz, *op. cit.*, p. 409.

For several years American Catholics have been debating with great earnestness the Catholic contribution to the intellectual life of America. One must recognize that such self-criticism is healthy; one must regret that in the discussion voices have sometimes become shrill and issues often beclouded.

For this reason Professor O'Dea's treatment is a welcome contribution. The book is written with the modesty of the scholar who makes clear that much of what he says is, of necessity, tentative. It also exhibits that sharpness of insight and mastery of his field which have earned Professor O'Dea a national reputation as a sociologist of religion.

The result is a book which will not completely please either party to the continuing debate. The author is constructing a series of hypotheses, and is concerned with pointing out areas where empirical research is sorely needed before we can fully understand our problems. Consequently his work avoids both free-swinging attack and headline-making exposure.

On the other hand, while recognizing that progress is being made, Professor O'Dea forthrightly sides with those who feel that there are still serious shortcomings in the American Catholic approach to the intellectual life, and that these shortcomings must be realistically examined.

His analysis, however, goes far beyond the American scene. He discusses the problem of the intellectual in any society, the specific problem of the Catholic intellectual of any time or place, and lastly the intellectual situation of contemporary American Catholicism.

Such a book reminds us that a group's capacity for self-examination is a sign of maturity. The example of figures such as Dante and St. Catherine of Siena remind us that such examination is also a sign of love.